SPLENDID REF.

40 Years of

Grass Parrakeet Husbandry

by Alec & Jo Mizen

SPLENDID REFLECTIONS

(the A to Z of breeding Splendid Grass Parrakeets)

Authors: Alec & Jo Mizen

Photography: Alec Mizen

Illustrations: Jo Mizen & Debra Nunn

Type-setting: Debra Nunn

Published by: Alec & Jo Mizen, Buckover Bird Sanctuary,
near Wotton-Under-Edge, Gloucestershire

Printed and bound by WBC Print Ltd, Bristol

*Any queries regarding the breeding or management of Splendids
may be addressed to the Authors (s.a.e., please)*

ISBN 0 9515345 0 5

A CIP catalogue record for this book is available from the British Library

CONTENTS

CONTENTS continued

Illustrations:

(Plants & Seeds enjoyed by Splendids)

Beech

Cotoneaster franchetii

Cotoneaster horizontalis

Dandelion

Elder

Firethorn

Groundsel

Millet Spray

Oregon Grape

Perennial Sow Thistle

Plantain

Raspberry

Rose

Rowan

Thistle

Line Drawings:

How to ring a Splendid

How to cut claws

FOREWORD

During the early part of 1950, my wife and I decided to expand our hobby of breeding Budgerigars and we built a range of aviaries in which to breed some of the Australian Parrakeets.

We visited a number of breeders and saw their stock, and were introduced to Mr W R Partridge of Evesham. On our first visit to his extensive establishment, we were suddenly confronted with a pair of the feathered gems, the **Splendid Grass Parrakeet**, *(Neophema Splendida)* and they certainly lived up to their name.

We ordered some and, as they were very expensive at the time, instead of purchasing the other varieties of Parrakeet we had intended, we saved up and, later that year, purchased two pairs. We were successful in breeding them in 6' x 3' x 3' aviaries and, since then, we have generally had one or two pairs in our mixed collections.

Around 1976 ill-health forced me to give up breeding birds and all our outside aviaries were demolished but, by 1978 my little upset was over and we decided to specialise in the breeding of Splendids in our bird-rooms.

Many visitors, friends and clients are always seeking information regarding the keeping and breeding of Splendids, so we decided to put our personal experiences down in book form and make it available to all who are interested.

We hope our efforts assist you in getting more pleasure and satisfaction from the delightful hobby of bird keeping and, perhaps, prevent you from falling into the occasional pitfalls we all meet.

SPLENDID REFLECTIONS
A and J Mizen
Buckover Bird Sanctuary
Gloucestershire
March 1989

AVIARIES

The discussions of whether to breed in aviaries or birdrooms will go on endlessly, but we feel it really depends on the personal preference or financial position of the fancier, as Splendids can be successfully bred in either.

Aviaries can be constructed of a whole variety of materials for the main framing, from wood to metal to plastic, with a small wire mesh covering. Generally, the size of mesh for Splendids would be ½" x ½", or ½" x 1". There does not appear to be any need to go smaller than this, as mice will gain entry to the aviary through any number of other small holes. Attached to the aviary should be a shelter within which feeding can be carried out.

An aviary constructed from rustic poles and of an irregular shape can give a very pleasing effect when it contains a small, mixed collection of various finches and one pair of Splendids but, if more than one pair are housed together, then fighting can occur.

For serious breeding, it is best to house one pair per aviary, with a flight size of about 6' x 2' 6" x 6' high and a shelter about 2' 6" x 2' 6" x 2' 6" at one end. These may be constructed in a range of two or three or a dozen if required, with an enclosed walkway behind the feeding shelters. A small pophole, about 6" square, would link the shelter to the flight, with a flap to enable you to shut the birds into the shelter on very cold and damp winter nights. If possible, an electric light could be used within the shelter area during the winter time to induce the birds to enter and have a longer feeding time. This light is a must if you run a group of cocks or hens together outside the breeding season, as quite often a dominant bird will guard the pophole and prevent any of the other birds from feeding during the day. Many birds are lost through this behaviour, if prevented from feeding for a few days.

It is advisable to have a small door to enable you to enter the flights from within the enclosed feeding area but, if this is impossible, fit a short, narrow door in the end of each flight, with an enclosed safety area running the whole length of the range.

ASPECT OF AVIARY

The siting of the aviary will be dictated by the size and position of your garden but, if possible, avoid a position where either a freezing North or North-East wind blows directly in, or where the boiling sun can create stifling conditions for the inmates. No bird likes to sit in the full sun all the time and, you may have noticed, very few of our native birds are in evidence during the hottest time of the day.

Nest boxes, if hung in the flight, should be in a position sheltered from the direct sun but also where the prevailing wind and rain cannot enter and make it uncomfortable for the Splendids.

Place the aviary where the birds can see people or animals approaching them from as far a distance as possible, so that they can fly to their favourite perching areas slowly, rather than be suddenly alarmed and, in their panic, collide with the aviary roof.

This action can so often result in the loss of young birds from a crushed skull or broken limb.

One of the drawbacks of breeding Splendids in aviaries is the habit of many of the shyer birds of disappearing from the flight when approached by the owners and their friends.

Perches are best made from natural branches, or Hazelnut wands, rather than rigid hardwood, which does not flex when a bird alights on it and can cause damage to legs and feet. Site the roosting perches as high as possible, but not too near the sides of the aviary where the inmates could be subjected to attacks by hawks or cats, etc. Roofs of ranges of aviaries are best covered with clear or obscure corrugated plastic sheets to prevent wild bird-droppings fouling the aviary floor. If a short section of sheeting is also fixed to the walls, enclosing part or all of the roosting perches, this would protect the Splendids from driving winds or rain.

Floors may be of gravel, concrete or slabs. If concrete or slabs are used, then provision must be made for a soakaway or drain, to allow the water and droppings to be flushed away when hosing or otherwise cleaning the floors, including a cover to prevent the birds from coming into contact with the stale food, or whatever may be collected within the drain. This cover would also prevent any vermin gaining admission to the aviary. We prefer gravel, to a depth of about 2"-3" thick, for floor covering. This can easily be removed when the area beneath the perches becomes soiled. Then the whole floor area can be cleared and gravel renewed periodically to prevent the build-up of any disease.

Floors of earth are not desirable but, as the birds spend much of their time on the ground it is advisable to have old pieces of logs dotted around for them to play on and chew. The planting of any shrubs is a waste of time - and a source of danger - as the Splendids would soon remove every leaf from the bushes. We have had a hen lose a leg by having a small twig coming into an aviary from outside. The bird was trapped by a leg ring sliding over the twig, whilst she was removing the leaves and bark. She was not discovered until evening, nearly dead and unable to get free. (Our vet was able to save her for us, however, and although she lost a leg, she remainded with us for a number of years and also bred some lovely youngsters.)

Beech
(Fagus)

Three examples of various types of Aviary

BIRDROOMS

Birdrooms come in many shapes and sizes, but are generally constructed of wood, bricks, or concrete blocks.

The needs of Splendids can be met in a building of any of these materials, providing that plenty of light is available and the room is damp- and draught-free, and vermin-proof.

Windows are generally on one side and breeding cages on the opposite wall. If the back wall is 6' high, then three rows of cages can be constructed, one above the other, with each of them being approximately 18½" high and a minimum of 5' long. Use two 24" x 15" cage fronts for each unit, with a panel of approximately 11" wide at one end, on which to hang the external nest box. We use a popular, national daily newspaper for floor covering, so the depth of each cage unit is made to fit, i.e. 18" from front to back. Below each cage front is a hinged panel to assist in cleaning out, and a length of hardboard 17" x 4" is placed beneath the perches to collect the droppings. These can be scraped off daily. A whole, open newspaper placed on the cage floor will allow soiled pages to be removed periodically without unduly upsetting the breeding pairs.

Slides are situated between each cage front, to separate the unit into smaller cages if required, say for catching any of the birds, and can be removed to make one long flight from adjoining breeding compartments. The area beneath the cages could be used as cupboards for storing show cages, pots, grits and nest boxes when not in use.

A shelf below the window acts as a worktop for the preparation of seed pots, etc., and seed can be stored beneath in containers.

A wire-mesh covered safety door or perch is desirable, in case a bird escapes from one of the breeding compartments into the bir-droom and, if the main door was open, it could be lost into the wild. It is also advis-able to cover the windows with wire-mesh, for the same reason.

Allow plenty of ventilation at all times, as the Splendid Parrakeet is a hardy little bird, if kept dry and not subjected to cold draughts. Electricity, we feel, is a must in the birdroom for lighting and, perhaps, a heating system to keep the room frost-free.

Flights adjoining the birdroom are desirable for the cocks and hens outside the breeding season if pairs are split up, and also for allowing your young Splendids to have plenty of exercise to develop, after being removed from the parents.

Site the birdroom so that the low morning sun enters and bathes the cages for a short while. The Splendids will enjoy this and the sun will have risen high enough to leave the cages in the shade, before it gets too hot and creates stifling condi-tions for sitting hens or chicks in the nest boxes.

The most vermin-proof floor for a birdroom is concrete, but it can also strike very cold during the wintertime. We prefer a wooden floor, set upon solid timber bearers, or short brick pillars. This allows access beneath the floor, so that we can place various baits for rats or mice, out of the reach of wild birds. If a concrete floor is used, it is better to have a wooden duckboard or mat to stand on whilst attending to your birds.

BUYING STOCK

If possible, visit a number of fanciers who breed Splendids and see for yourself the difference between strains of birds. They vary a lot, even within one collection.

There appear to be at least two species - one with a short bib, the other with a much deeper one. Indeed, some have been bred with almost a complete red front. Mutations have appeared; Blues, both white- and orange-breasted, are available, along with others, and the choices are becoming more numerous each year. Many of these newcomers are very expensive, but are available if anyone desires to obtain them.

Decide which type of Splendid "fills your eye" and obtain, if possible, two unrelated pairs. If you have only one pair and they do not prove to be compatible, a complete season may be wasted but, with two unrelated pairs, the birds can be swapped around.

When you visit other fanciers, you will notice one or two birds which stand out head and shoulders above the others. Do not expect to buy these as they are, in many cases, the result of many years' work and will be the first line stock breeders for the following year. If the owner of these birds has been following a recorded breeding programme, it may be possible to buy birds from the same lines and thereby breed - if Lady Luck smiles upon you - youngsters of a like nature. In all forms of stock breeding, brothers and sisters of prize-winning exhibits, whilst perhaps not showing the same qualities themselves, are perfectly capable of breeding similar - or even better - prize-winners.

The first thing to go by when purchasing stock is the bird's eyes. The bird should be alert and the eyes clear and shining. If the bird is into a full or partial moult, the feathers may be spiky or rough-looking with a few missing around the face, but these should soon grow again, leaving the Splendid once more in a sparkling condition. Any sign of stickiness around the beak, eyes or vent should be viewed with caution, as should any bird which stands on a perch or in a corner with both feet down, head under wing and feathers all puffed up into a ball. Splendids, or any other birds, in this condition can be made by their owners to become alert for a short while, possibly by a short, sharp noise or by rattling the cage bars, but will very soon return to their original condition of ailing. In our experience - over about forty years of breeding many varieties of birds, as well as Splendid Grass Parrakeets - we have noticed that, in general, fit Splendids will sleep with their head under their wing, but standing on one leg only.

Ensure that the Splendids on offer are of pure Splendid blood and not the result of cross-breeding with other species of Grass Parrakeet. Sometimes, when there have been odd birds - say Turquoisines and Splendids - available, it has been known for fanciers to pair them up and produce young, some of which are fertile and able to completely ruin anyone's serious attempts to breed a useful strain of either bird.

At the same time as purchasing your stock, enquire about the feeding methods and mixtures being fed to the Splendids at that time, and purchase some of the seed mixtures to take home with you. Mix this with an equal amount of your own seed mixture, thereby slowly acclimatising your birds to their new food.

Before purchasing stock for your aviaries or birdroom, however, it would help if you had decided on the number of birds you can easily manage to attend to. We are all, I think, liable to make a mistake when visiting a fellow fancier's establishment on a nice, sunny day to view the ranges of aviaries, or breeding pairs in birdrooms. We feel we would like to copy what we see, but often do not stop to imagine the same scene on a bitterly cold, mid-winter's day. For birds in aviaries it gets dark around 4 o'clock in the evening and it is still dark when you leave for work in the morning. The only times, therefore, to view and enjoy your Splendids, would be at weekends and an ailing bird could possibly be lost, unless your spouses are as interested as you are in looking after them.

With birds in birdrooms or with large, well-lit shelters, this would not be the case, but they would still need attending to however you feel, or whatever the weather. It would be very easy for the great enjoyment and satisfaction we all feel in keeping and attending to our stock, to change into unwanted drudgery should sickness strike and you have over-extended yourself.

When you require further stock to increase or improve your stud, return, if possible, to the fancier from whom you originally purchased your birds, or to a person who is breeding from the same strain. In doing so, you should find that the new purchases will blend with the ones you have, without throwing out too many birds that do not approach your standard.

Select the intended purchase which excels in the particular feature you consider is required within your own stud and, by following a prepared plan of line breeding, you will be able to spread this feature throughout your young Splendids.

If possible, take with you on your visit one of your own birds with which to compare the intended purchase, as we can so often buy a new bird that appears to be perfectly able to fulfil our desires, only to arrive home with it and place it among our own stock and find it is inferior. This simple strategy can often save you much disappointment.

Many years ago, when we were in the ranks of Budgerigar Beginner Breeders, we were warned of the practice used by the odd, unscrupulous dealer who would use a special show cage that had been reduced in size by about ¼" all round, to show birds to prospective purchasers. Any reasonably-sized bird exhibited in this cage would appear, to the untrained eye, to be a real "stormer", until it was taken home and compared with one's own stock!

We never experienced this practice at any time in our own dealings with numerous members of the fancy, but would occasionally have this information repeated for our "protection". Needless to say, we always took along one of our own, standard-sized Budgie show cages, in which to view our prospective purchase.

BREEDING CONDITION

This is a term so often used - but seldom explained to beginners - in keeping and breeding Splendids. It is very often mistaken for show condition, which is generally almost immediately after a moult, when the birds are wearing their complete new coats and are feather-perfect. A fair number of birds around would not dream of doing anything like breeding and get their nice, new clothes mucky, but obviously some will. A hen in breeding condition would be far more likely to try and sit in the water-pot than stand still on a perch for a judge!

Splendids in breeding condition need not necessarily be in perfect feather condition, but the cocks will be found feeding a hen if one will stay still long enough. They will run or bob in little, jerky steps beneath the perch of their selected mate, spreading their tails in a beautifully-shaped yellow, green and black fan, all the while making a little piping song.

Any other cock seen nearby will be driven away and sometimes quite a tussle can ensure, with injuries being caused between evenly-matched antagonists.

They will continuously feed their hens by regurgitation - that is, bringing back partly-digested food from their crops - or even presenting to the hen a large sunflower seed, which they may both eat from either end. He will only allow his particular hen to feed from their chosen food-pots and will attempt to climb on her back at every opportunity.

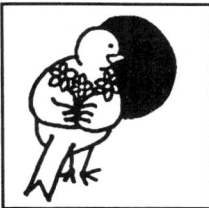

If a nest-box is nearby, he will be perching at the entrance, spreading his tail, calling to attract the hen, and will appear to be giving himself a dry bath by continually fluffing up his feathers, shaking himself, and peering into the entrance.

The hen, in breeding condition, will have lost her teenage-type coquettishness of flying up to any male, sometimes letting herself be fed, but spurning any other attentions that are being made to her, and flying away before things get too serious! Her figure will have changed slightly from a slim young thing to a fuller, almost matronly, shape. She will be investigating any and all orifices that remotely appear to be used as, or could be enlarged into, a nest hole. In our breeding units, she will spend hours chewing up the newspaper floor-covering, fluffing up her rump feathers and attempting to place the chewed paper, sunflower seed shells, or anything else she can find, under her feathers. These will be locked down once more and she will fly to the nest-box and line her nest with her treasures.

She will approach a cockbird and call, like a nestling, to be fed. After this, with eyes receding to pinhead size, she will crouch across the perch in open invitation to her mate to cover her.

After a few days, due to the changes within her body to allow for the formation and passing of eggs, her droppings will be noticed to have enlarged considerably and she will be seen, sitting on the perch, her slim, tapered figure gone and her tail pumping with increasing speed.

Within a short while, she will disappear into her nest-box and later emerge, having laid her egg, to rejoin the cock Splendid, who will joyously announce to all and sundry, "What a clever chap I am!"

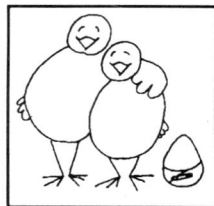

BREEDING

Both birds of the pair must be fit and ready for breeding. This can occur at any time of the year in the birdroom and the thermostat in ours is set for about 40°F. The heat is only used when our birds are breeding and laying during the very cold winter months and just keeps the room frost-free. This, we find, helps to prevent egg-binding among young hens.

Splendids can still be in good breeding condition even if they are in a partial moult and you will find the cocks, if kept together, calling and chasing each other around the aviaries, trying to make territories for themselves. The hens will be exploring every corner they can, tearing up newspaper into shreds, and often chewing everything in sight.

Make sure you have enough seed and other supplies in hand to feed your stock throughout the whole of the breeding season, as many a clutch of young birds has been lost through a change of seed or rearing food halfway through the rearing period.

Spend a little time studying your birds, noticing the various points about each one, which makes it appear desirable in your eyes. Then, unless it forms a brother/sister relationship, decide which birds to pair together. Try not to pair two birds together which possess the same, glaring faults; for example, a beak that juts out from the bird's head at right angles, instead of being nicely tucked-in. If one breeds with two birds, each of which exhibits such a defect, you can only expect a fair proportion of your young birds to show this up in varying degrees. The same thing applies with good points, as often "like begets like".

Don't attempt breeding with more than one pair of Splendids per aviary or cage. One may be lucky enough to obtain pairs which are compatible for a short while, but if one hen enters the nest-box of another containing eggs or chicks, then a bloodbath may ensue.

If breeding in a long range of aviaries or flights, do not house Splendids in adjoining compartments, but fill every other one with birds of a different species. Even with long-established pairs, you will find birds with a "wandering eye" for a mate in the next compartment and fights will occur, resulting in lost eyes or toes. Double-wiring can be used between adjoining flights, and it may stop injuries, but on occasions they will still attempt to attack each other, resulting in unfilled eggs and wasted breeding seasons. Generally, there is very little trouble, but it is better to be wise before the event, rather than afterwards. Having unrelated pairs will enable you to either make up more pairs from your youngsters, or sell unrelated pairs to other fanciers. The Splendids will soon deteriorate, both in size and vigour, if brother and sister pairings are made. Don't forget that unseen possible defects, as well as desirable visible attributes, can both be passed down to the offspring.

When breeding in aviaries, late in April, hang up your nest-boxes but do not allow the birds entry to them for a few more days. By this time the pair should have settled down, with the cock feeding, and possibly mating with, the hen. It is not advisable to commence breeding in the open before this, because every year we get a very cold spell around mid-April, when the wild Sloe or Blackthorn bush is in flower, and if young hens especially are commencing to lay, egg-binding (or failure to expel the egg) can ensue, with the possible loss of your hen.

If egg-binding does occur, you will find your hen generally on the floor in a corner, with an upraised rump, pumping wildly and looking like a bedraggled ball of feathers. The best treatment we have found for this is to place the poor mite in a hospital cage or show cage in a quiet spot, and apply gentle warmth to the floor of the cage. We have placed the cage atop, or in front of, a warm radiator and in most cases, if the bird has been noticed in time, the egg will be laid within a few hours. Allow her a few days to acclimatise to the outdoor temperature before placing her back in the aviary, but it is advisable to prevent her from breeding until later in the year.

Small amounts of bread and milk, or a ready-mixed rearing food, should be offered soon after pairing and this will be explained in more detail under the heading "Feeding".

In our experience, one-year-old hens breed perfectly well with little trouble, but young cocks rarely succeed in fertilising their eggs for the first round. This does, however, give the hen a chance to sit for the desired 18-20 days, and completely recover from laying one set of eggs, before beginning her cycle once more almost immediately when clear eggs are removed.

If the eggs are fertile, with the eggs taking on a pearly lustre, do not be in a hurry to discard them if they fail to hatch after the normal 18-20 days from the first egg, as we have known them to take up to an extra week or more to hatch in cold weather. We have often found that the hen does not sit until the third egg has been laid. A clutch can consist of four to seven eggs. More than this number is unusual.

Keep an eye on the hen in the nest-box and you will notice the chicks are hatching by the behaviour of the cock Splendid calling - virtually asking you for some of its favourite soft food, and also by the appearance of eggs shells in the corner of the box. This is the time to feed titbits, little and often.

At first, when the chicks are hatching, the hen appears rarely to leave the box for food. The cock will be observed busily feeding and making periodic visits to the nest-box, in which he will regurgitate partially-digested food for the hen. The hen will then later feed the tiny chicks by turning each one onto its back among the unhatched eggs and pumping the milky, crop fluid into the chick. After about a week or so the older chicks will receive the food from the cock, with the hen continuing to feed the youngest.

The baby chicks are born covered in a white, downy fluff and by about a fortnight old will be beginning to show signs of feathering. At this stage of growth the hen will leave the nest-box for increasing lengths of time during the day, with the cock taking over more responsibility for feeding the chicks. The hen, however, will continue to brood the chicks overnight.

When the young are between a month and five weeks old they will begin to leave the nest-box. On odd occasions one or more will leave the box before this, ejected by its companions pushing and shoving to be at the box entrance to receive food from the parent birds. It is advisable to place odd, twiggy branches or the like at the end of the flights, as young birds leaving the nest-box for the first time will fly crashing into everything before they eventually gain control over their flight. Many young birds can receive injuries at this time.

Young birds bred in birdrooms do not have such a large area to fly in so, although they will crash about on leaving the nest-box, they do not have a long distance in which to gain enough speed to cause themselves much damage.

In our experience, the young Splendids can be left with their parents until a few days before the next clutch of eggs is due to hatch and the cock will continue to feed them without any trouble at all but, if a young cock shows any signs of red on its breast on leaving the nest-box, the parent cock may attack it at any time.

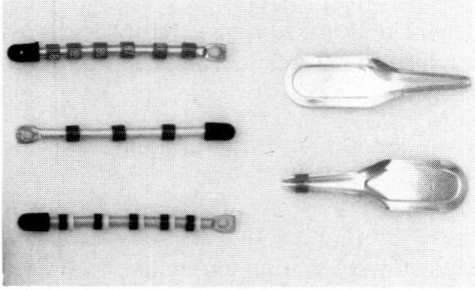

When they are removed from the parents, we like to ring the young with coloured, split-plastic identifying rings, before placing them with other young birds or odd cock birds to develop in their own time and eventually moult out.

As soon as you can identify cocks from hens, it is best if the sexes are housed in separate enclosures to prevent fighting or premature bonding. Hens - generally, but not always - have a row of white spots on the underside of each wing. Young cocks occasionally display a few of these spots but nearly always lose them when they have completely moulted.

On occasions, some Splendids will be completely disinterested in their partners and make no attempt to feed each other or to mate. If, after a few weeks or so, no movement has been made towards entering the nest-box or working within it, it is a good idea to split the pair and give each one a different partner. If this is impossible, owing to lack of available substitutes, try parting the birds for a week or two and then try them again, possibly in a different location. This works on some occasions; also moving around or changing the nest-box can sometimes trigger off the breeding cycle with some pairs.

Splendids which have been bred in aviaries can sometimes prove to be quite unsuitable for breeding in birdrooms, owing to their nervousness at being in such close proximity with their keeper and unable to escape to a place of hiding. Some of these will eventually settle down, but it would not be advisable to interfere with their nest-box in any way. The birds panic when the box is opened and, in scrabbling to escape through the pophole, eggs can be scattered and broken, or young chicks injured or killed.

One of the interests in breeding any form of livestock is the challenge to succeed. It is not just a question of placing two birds together, supplying them with seed and water, and periodically removing young. Some years you will find that, no matter what system you use, nothing will go right for you, but these not-too-frequent periods will be forgotten and amply rewarded when you enter your aviary or birdroom one day and see one or more delightful, bright-eyed and tight-feathered young Splendids gazing at you from their perch alongside a very proud parent.

When breeding in cages or aviaries, it is preferable to place both cock and hen in at the same time. This will prevent either bird from deciding it is their own territory and attempting to exclude the other from the shelter or feeding areas.

Millet Spray

COMPATIBILITY

The temperament of Splendids, as with people, can be very varied. On the one hand you can get the odd cock or hen which is so bad-tempered it will allow nothing to approach its territory and will drive away, or even kill, a mate who is introduced to it. On the other hand, you will find single birds or pairs which will adopt and rear any number of foster chicks with no trouble at all. This type is worth its weight in gold. The first type is useless for breeding and is able only to be placed in a mixed aviary with a group of inmates who are well able to look after themselves!

The large majority of Splendids fall into various groups between the last two. One can find both dominant cocks and hens being kept with groups of either sex which, in full breeding condition, will attempt to obtain their own territory around the feed pots, etc., but their actions can soon be spotted and the birds paired up and moved to a flight or breeding unit of their own, where they should soon go down with eggs.

If one should be unfortunate enough to lose either of a pair with young, do not attempt to introduce another mate until the young are old enough to be removed from the remaining parent. A few days after the removal of the young and nest-box, a new mate could be introduced and will probably be accepted.

CLEANLINESS

A line must be drawn between clinical conditions and the pile of droppings beneath the bird's favourite spot nearly reaching the perch! The system we use in our birdrooms entails the use of five or six sheets of newspaper covering the cage floor, with a slide of hardboard beneath each perch. These slides can be removed and scraped clean every day or so to remove the large droppings from the laying or brooding hen. The food and water containers are taken out and the top, soiled sheet of newspaper removed each week.

When the young hatchlings leave the nest, there are still husks and some seed on the floor, as well as in the pots, for them to pick over and the remaining sheets can be removed when the young are taken away from their parents. The breeding unit can then be completely cleaned out, newspapers replaced with little fuss and the pair allowed to continue breeding once more.

CLUBS & SOCIETIES

Almost all towns or counties have their own clubs or Cage Bird Societies. Some of these are specialist clubs for a particular species or group, whilst others cater for all breeds.

Anyone thinking of starting their own bird breeding programme would be well advised to join a local club, where they would meet many others of a like mind and would be able to add to their knowledge through discussions with individual fanciers or by attending any of the specialist talks and lectures that are a feature of so many clubs.

Local club and larger shows are held, many of which are advertised in the magazine "*Cage and Aviary Birds*" and, by attending or showing at these, one can pick up many useful ideas - not the least of which is what type of bird is held in great esteem by the various judges. Whether you wish to show your Splendids or not, it will enable you to select the type of birds to form your own stud. Remember, it costs no more to breed first class stock than it does to breed rubbish. Through meeting other breeders, you will be able to discover who else in your area breeds a good type of Splendid and, no doubt, you will get many invitations to visit other fanciers' collections to view the birds and get much helpful advice on setting up your aviary or birdroom and purchasing stock.

Some clubs also bulk-buy seed, etc., and a member may be able to purchase these articles at discount prices.

Visits are arranged to other clubs and to attend social functions and you are able to extend your circle of friends among the members of these clubs.

Most clubs put on shows of various kinds and interested members are generally welcome to assist at these events. There is so much to be done, from checking the exhibits in and out, to assisting the judges by bringing the birds in their respective classes to the judging table and returning them later, when they would eventually be staged, resplendent, with their coloured cards and brilliant rosettes.

Most club members, in our experience, are only too pleased to assist newcomers in any way and generally one or two may have some second-hand showcages for sales. Purchasing these and painting them up will work out much cheaper than buying new ones.

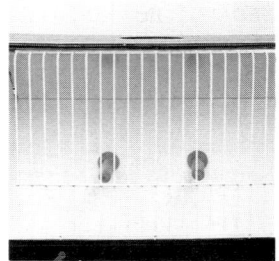

There is much hard work and dedication involved in benching the bird that wins the coveted top awards at any show, and many fanciers drop out of showing before they reach the summit. If, at any time, through any reason, one decides to concentrate on any other aspects of birdkeeping and discontinue with showing, the financial outlay will have been far less with reconditioned apparatus than by purchasing new equipment right from the start.

You can be assured, however, that the thrill of visiting a show after the judges have completed their task, and finding your Splendid in its showcage, festooned with rosettes, is well worth the effort. It is inadvisable, however, to show birds from outside aviaries as, being housed for a couple of days in a warm hall during midwinter and then being released back into a cold, outside aviary, could really upset your Splendids, if not kill them.

One of the things that impresses me about the clubs in which we have been involved, is the fact that no-one is too old to learn new tricks and every member, new or old, has something to offer. Perhaps, if there are enough people interested, a club or specialist society may be formed to cater solely for Splendid Grass Parrakeet breeders, with rosettes or cash prizes being awarded at shows where there is a class for Splendids.

DESCRIPTION

A cock Splendid Grass Parrakeet is a truly magnificent little bird and many people, seeing one for the first time, are often lost for words. The head and sides of the neck are shining cobalt blue, shading into green on the back and edges of the chest. The main chest area is scarlet, cut off in a line from the bird's yellow underbelly. The scarlet area varies from a short bib, to the whole of the chest and belly. The wings are blue and green above and black beneath, with a black leading edge and flight feathers. The tail feathers are blue-green and black, with the outer ones of yellow. The eyes are brown and the beak is black.

Young birds generally lack the scarlet breast. The head is of varying shades of blue, the beak is of a light brown colour and young cocks are almost purple over the brow. The hen Splendid is predominantly green, with the lower belly being yellow. The head is of a much lighter blue than that of the cock,

as are the leading edges of the wings. The scarlet breast of the cock is missing and is replaced by an olive-green colour, cut off in a similar straight line from the yellow beneath. In our experience, hens generally carry a row of white spots on the underside of the wings.

The hens of Splendids and Turquoisines could, if taken singly, be mistaken for each other but, placed side by side, the Turquoisine hen's greens and blues are of a deeper colour than those of the Splendid.

There is quite a difference in the depth of colour when different strains of Splendid cocks are observed and this is an attribute that has been achieved by selective breeding, rather than mutations. The young birds have their first moult at about four to six months old and the cocks get their first red breast and deep blue head at this time. This area of deep blue becomes larger with each successive moult and the bird does not normally achieve its full colouring until it is about two years old. The size of cocks and hens is comparable to a slimline present-day Budgerigar - about 8-8½" long.

Their range in the wild is confined generally to the dry, open spaces of Central and Western Australia, where they feed on the various varieties of grass seeds. Spinifex seed appears to be its favourite and, where this plant abounds, so the numbers of Splendid Grass Parrakeets increase. It appears to rely mainly on the dew from the plants for its water supply, rarely visiting the area's waterholes.

The song of the Splendid is soft - almost a whistle - which, although with no stretch of the imagination could it be called melodious, is not unpleasant or penetrating. Its warning call is a single, high-pitched note, repeated often.

DEAD IN SHELL

This is something we all experience at some time or other during our breeding of Splendids. It has been put down to various causes; lack of magnesium, the so-called "Lethal Factor" of certain pairings, mineral or vitamin deficiency, or incorrect humidity, etc.

We suffered originally from this trouble when we used large, deep nest-boxes with two or three inches of rotten wood or damp sawdust in the bottom. We noticed that when we opened the nest-box for inspection, the hen would be sitting on a clutch of eggs in one spot, with one or two eggs having rolled away from her. We marked these eggs and discovered, on subsequent inspections, a similar situation with the eggs but the marked eggs were now under the hen and different, unmarked eggs scattered. As this appeared to be happening each time the hen left the box to defecate, it is probable that the eggs had been left uncovered for long periods after the embryo had started to grow. We altered the design of our nest-boxes (to be discussed later), added a small, concave base, and we now seldom find dead in shell.

It is best to refrain from handling the eggs for any purpose as it is so easy to transfer any infection from your hands to the eggs. This will probably pass through the shell and into the sterile interior, resulting in the death of the embryo at any stage. It can be seen how a whole birdroom or series of aviaries could become infected, with the subsequent increase of dead in shell.

The humidity within the birdroom or nest-box could be too high or too low. We have found that the level needs to be around 55%, ± 10%, humidity.

All these causes, together with others, could contribute towards the dead in shell rate but, if we attend to feeding our Splendids a balanced diet, keeping our flights and birdrooms well-ventilated and, perhaps, investigating a little less the nest-boxes containing eggs and laying hens, we should manage to keep our losses to a minimum.

When pairing your birds, examine their feet and clip off the sharp points found on any of their toenails to prevent eggs being punctured. Great care must be taken not to cut into the vein running down the nails, which can be seen by holding the foot up into the light.

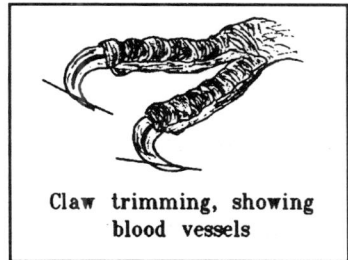

Claw trimming, showing blood vessels

DISABLED FANCIERS

It is possible for many disabled people to achieve the great pleasures of breeding the delightful little Splendid Grass Parrakeet.

Either a room in the house or a 6' x 4' garden shed, with a door on one long side, may be utilised. One 4' long double breeding cage can be fixed along each end, at a height which will enable the birds to be attended to whilst sitting on a chair or in a wheelchair. A nest-box can be mounted either over a cage front door or on a wooden panel at one end. The central slide could be temporarily fixed in position, keeping the birds at one end whilst the seed and water, etc., are replenished at the other. In this way there will be less chance of any escapees.

To remove any young birds, an old show cage or similar could be hung onto an open doorway for a few days and a piece of millet spray placed inside. This will induce the young birds to investigate the cage and get used to entering it. When you wish to catch the birds, they will not be frightened to enter, if slowly coaxed in. With the small cage removed, it will be a reasonably easy task to catch the birds inside, without too much distress to them.

Members of your local societies, I am sure, would be only too pleased to help someone unable to construct the various small aids that may be required to get over any particular difficulty experienced whilst attending to your birds.

Perhaps readers of *"Cage & Aviary Birds"*, through the medium of "Letters to the Editor" have ideas regarding the adaptation of any birdroom equipment, which may be of use to a disabled fancier.

Plantain
(Plantago)

ELECTRICITY IN THE BIRDROOM OR AVIARY

During the winter many Splendids are lost, owing to being unable to eat enough food to sustain themselves through the long hours of darkness from about 4 p.m. until 8 a.m. the following morning. They become frightened to enter a dark, closed shelter, or are disturbed by perhaps a passing car or house light. It is also possible for them to remain outside the shelter under freezing cold and wet conditions.

In a range of aviaries two or three small, low-wattage night-lights would be sufficient to attract the birds into the shelters to feed and roost, especially whilst feeding an early round of chicks.

In the birdroom it is possible to have full lighting, together with heating if desired. Our lights are on a time-switch and come on at 7 a.m., so the birds are well awake and feeding when visited a short time later. The lights go off around 9 a.m. and, during the winter, come on again at 4 p.m. A dimmer switch is manually operated around 9 p.m., which leaves a small night light to allow the Splendids to regain their perches or nest-boxes if frightened during the hours of darkness.

We have found that, by using lights in this fashion, our birds come into breeding condition much earlier than when they were in unlighted aviaries and we can usually begin pairing up in February. We also have a low-wattage heating system that is capable of keeping the birdroom frost-free when the hens are laying and, in this way, we seldom experience any egg binding among our birds.

Out of the breeding season our birdrooms have gone down to -12°C on one occasion during early 1982 and the birds suffered no ill-effects. Splendids are perfectly hardy, if well fed and given dry and snug overnight accommodation.

Many different types of burglar alarm are now on the market for people who feel they are necessary to protect their stock. These range from the elaborate infra-red type, which detect any movement; pressure pads under various floor coverings; or window and door micro-switches, to the "Welcome Home" type now available. This last type of detector will detect body heat and movement over various distances and switch on a light or alarm when activated. One of ours was regularly triggered off by a cat and a hedgehog, until adjusted to allow for creatures of this size. It wasn't very amusing to be awakened in the early hours and confronted with a hedgehog trundling across the lawn, quite oblivious to the commotion it was causing.

It is virtually impossible to recommend any particular type, as each aviary or birdroom location will offer a different problem.

Check with the various firms offering this equipment and make sure that the type you choose has the following:

1.   A back-up battery incorporated, to take over in the event of a power failure.

2.   If using a flood-lighting system incorporating a light-sensitive cell to make the unit inoperative after first light, make sure you have a second circuit to operate an alarm during the hours of daylight because, during the summer months, the light-sensitive type may only be switched on for a few hours overnight.

3.   Use hidden or protected cabling to your detecting units, to avoid them being discovered or disabled.

EQUIPMENT

All of us, I believe, collect various bits and pieces of equipment, either manufactured or self-constructed. Two pieces we would not like to be without are a hospital cage and the ionisation unit, both used in the birdroom.

The hospital cage can be purchased from one of the various appliance manufacturers advertising in popular bird-fancier's periodicals, or constructed from a Budgie-type show cage or a single breeding cage with a false, perforated metal floor and two low-wattage bulbs mounted beneath. A sheet of glass should be fixed over the wire front, leaving a ventilation space at the top. A small thermometer must be fixed inside. The two bulbs, when switched on, will speedily bring the temperature within the cage up to around 80°F, when one may be switched off. The remaining one should keep the cage interior nicely heated without being excessive.

Another way of providing heat for a sick bird is to hang up a type of ceramic heat lamp, used in rearing chickens, to the front of the cage near the perch. You will find that the bird will approach as close to the lamp as possible at first but, as it recovers, it will move away from the lamp until it obviously no longer requires it.

In all electrical installations, get the assistance of an expert in that field to, at the very least, inspect the finished job and test it before use. When using a manufactured hospital cage, follow the instructions for use carefully, as the metal used in the construction of some may become quite hot.

The ioniser we have fitted in the ceiling of our birdroom keeps it virtually free from dust and the distinctive smell of seed. It needs to have the needle regularly cleaned, together with the outside of the unit, as it seems to attract the dust to itself and other surfaces nearby. Wiping these surfaces clean is a very small price to pay for the very pleasant atmosphere created elsewhere in the room.

All seed to be used should be kept in closed, vermin-proof containers, as mouse urine can prove fatal if contaminated seed is fed to your stock. A dustbin - regularly emptied and cleaned - for soiled newspapers and scrapings from slides, is a very useful addition to any birdroom. It gives one great satisfaction to enter a tidy, but obviously working, birdroom and it can very often mean the difference between a visitor purchasing one of your surplus stock or moving to another fancier to satisfy his or her requirements.

We feed all our seed mixtures and water in open, plastic flower-pot saucers. The Splendids, on the whole, take great delight in bathing and we find it also helps to keep the nest-box humid if the hen enters with wet feathers. The water and seed pots are replenished at least once daily, so they are always nice and fresh.

On the front of each external nest-box are two small pins. On one pin are the coloured, plastic split-rings for all young from the pair within the cage. The young birds are rung when they are removed from their parents. On the other pin is hung a circular disc, red on one side and yellow on the other. On entering the birdroom one can easily see at a glance which nest-boxes contained eggs - yellow disc showing - or young birds, red disc. A simple piece of equipment, but it saves a lot of time. We use 4-pint, plastic milk containers, from which we replenish our seed pots, and the top half of a plastic lemonade bottle makes a fine funnel when filling containers.

One piece of equipment which is a must for any fancier is a hand-net for catching birds which are either loose in the birdroom or in an aviary. The nets we use are home-made and are 18" in diameter. We use a heavy-gauge

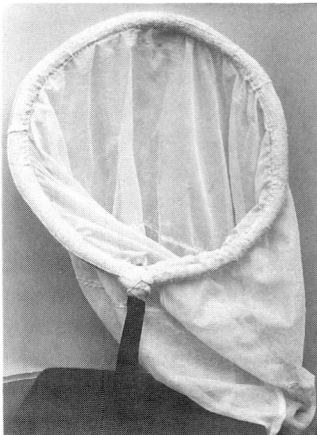

fencing wire, which is bent to form a circle, together with an integral short handle. The whole of this is padded with thin foam-rubber to make the "O" ring about 1" thick and the handle more comfortable to hold. (Padding is essential around the net entrance, as you will find it impossible to prevent a bird from being knocked by it at some time or another.) The body itself is of nylon netting, sewn to form a triangular enclosure approximately 2' from mouth to tail, with the mouth large enough to be sewn around and firmly fixed to the wire frame. We find that, with a net as large as this, it is not unwieldy and there is much less likelihood of discomfort to any bird through coming into contact with it. If Splendids in aviaries have to be caught, it is better to reduce the numbers flying around by directing as many as possible into the smaller shelter first. You will cause less stress to other birds in adjoining flights if they also can be shut into their shelters or you will find that, by using a net in one flight, it will cause utter chaos among the surrounding ones. Great care must be taken at the time of catching the Splendids because the odd one or two will insist on flying to the floor and running around. Whilst you are intent on catching a specific bird with the net, it would be easy to inadvertently step on one of these.

When catching birds in cages it is advisable to completely empty them of food and water containers and then direct the birds, singly, into as small an area as possible, using slides, before using a cupped hand to achieve your purpose.

One of the joys of visiting other fanciers' premises is being able to see the various home-made tools or appliances in use. I have quite often seen something quite simple in a beginner's birdroom - perhaps a clip to hold cuttlefish to the cage wall - and have wondered why no-one else had thought of it.

A quite simple seed winnower can be made from a rectangular cardboard box, with a baffle fixed a third of the way along the inside and reaching about two-thirds of the box height. A small hole is made on the end of the box, near the top of the smallest section.

With the top of the box almost covered, locate the hose from a vacuum cleaner's blowing end over the small hole, and slowly pour your mixture of seed and husks through the stream of air and into the small section. If the vacuum hose is located correctly, the majority of the light debris will be blown from the seed, over the baffle and into the largest section of the box. Repeat the action two or three times and the seed should be clean enough to be offered to your birds once more. Trial and error with the hose will give you the correct location for entry of the air into the box.

Under *no* circumstances use seed recleaned in this manner if there is the remotest chance of any of your stock being ill, as it is far better to discard all spilt seed than to risk the possibility of infection and possible loss of any bird. For individual seed pots, the pot can be agitated to bring the light husks uppermost and, holding the pot over a dustbin, gently blow the husks away manually. Emptying the remaining seed and dust into a household flour sieve and shaking will remove all or most of the small particles. This is the method we use and, in this way, the used seed from one pair is never mixed with that from another.

We find a small vacuum cleaner called a "Dustbuster" is invaluable when cleaning out the cages at the end of the breeding season. It enables us to remove all the dust from cage corners, etc., before we repaint the birdroom and cages.

EGG BINDING

On occasions during the winter, if the weather has been unusually mild or if the feeding system used has brought the birds into breeding condition early, the hen Splendids will commence to lay, either on the floor of the aviary or in the birdroom. As our winters can be so unreliable, it is not prudent to allow the hen to enter a nest-box in the flight much before mid-April, as a cold snap during her laying period could result in egg-binding. This is a condition in which the hen is unable to pass the egg owing to cold, immaturity or cramp, along with other possible causes. She will generally be found, huddled in a corner of the aviary or cage in a very distressed condition. She must be removed immediately to a dimly-lit and heated environment where, after a short while, she eventually passes the egg. The Splendid hen must be slowly acclimatised once more to living in unheated conditions and, personally, we would not allow her to stay out in the aviary again until the weather warmed up.

Various other methods have been advocated in the past to assist the hen, such as administering olive oil to the vent with a soft brush but, if the egg should be broken in any way, it will more than probably result in the death of the hen. Not being qualified in the veterinary field, we do not believe in dabbling but, if you are in any doubt, call in the services of a vet.

If breeding in a birdroom is practiced, it is possible to have the quarters slightly heated during the laying period and this generally - but not always - assists in preventing egg-binding.

We have found heat to be the most beneficial treatment in most cases of illness and, in the case of egg-binding, keeping a bird in a temperature approaching 85°F has resulted in the successful passing of the egg.

Should it be found that egg-binding persists among your stock, attention should be paid to the adequate provision of supplementary feeding, as a mineral deficiency of, say manganese, could aggravate the condition.

EGG LAYING

When breeding in aviaries where the sealed nest-box has been in position since the previous breeding season, it will be found that eggs will be laid, normally within a couple of weeks at the latest. If the pair has bred before, egg-laying will commence within a few days, provided both birds are in breeding condition. We found that, if pairs in outside aviaries had not produced eggs by the 20th May, then those same pairs were unlikely to breed that year. This has not applied whilst breeding in birdrooms.

Eggs are laid every other day until the full clutch of four to seven eggs is reached. On rare occasions up to nine eggs have been laid by hens owned by us, but the last two of three in a clutch of this size generally become so encrusted with droppings that they fail to hatch.

The hen generally begins to sit after laying the second egg. The first two young can be expected to hatch around the 20th/21st day from the date the first egg is laid, with successive young being hatched at two-day intervals. Hens being individuals, though, this is not always the case, as we have known the first couple of eggs to be a week overdue and still hatch out. The hen, instead of sitting tight, has spent her time standing over the eggs and not allowing them to reach the correct temperature for the embryo to commence germination until later than normal.

We have not found that the size of the egg has much bearing on the eventual size of the young Splendids produced but, quite often, one will find a noticeable difference in size of the young in the same nest, from eggs that appeared to be of identical size. Perhaps some of the young are more likely to induce the parents to feed them than their siblings.

EYE INFECTIONS

Some Splendids are prone to eye infections on occasions. The birds are inclined to wipe their beaks on perches or cage fronts after feeding and, if soft food has been available to them, particles of this can adhere to these surfaces. If the beak cleaning has been carried out in an over-energetic manner, some of these particles can be rubbed off onto other birds' faces or eyes. This will entail further face-rubbing, resulting in any material from soiled perches, etc., possibly entering and damaging the eyes or causing infection.

All perches and other favourite beak- and face-wiping areas must be scraped, washed, cleaned or replaced regularly to keep any possible infection of this kind to a minimum.

Our vet prescribed *Chloromycetin Ophthalmic* ointment, available only on veterinary prescription, for one of our birds which had an eye condition. The bird was separated from its companions and treated, and within a short while the infection was cleared. (Needless to say, all the old perches were burned and the flight cage washed down and disinfected on the removal of the ailing bird.)

We always believe that it is unwise to treat any bird that falls sick without first consulting a veterinary surgeon, as it is so easy for an untrained person to mistake a symptom of something potentially serious for something minor. It is false economy to risk your entire stud in this fashion.

The safest way to keep your stud of Splendids healthy is to watch out for the first sign of any sickness during your daily ministerings to them. Isolate the bird immediately - don't wait "a few days to see if anything will develop" whilst it is still in the company of its fellows, and begin any treatment as soon as you are sure there is anything that needs attention.

Rose
(Rosa)

FEATHER TEXTURE

There is a marked difference in the feather texture of most, if not all, species of bird. The light, soft feathers usually to be found on the smaller birds are called "yellows". On many of the larger birds a larger, coarser type of feather texture is often encountered, giving the bird a less neat appearance, and this type of bird is called a "buff".

It would be unwise, when attempting to form a stud of Splendids, to continuously breed birds of the same feather texture together, as it could possibly lead to a complete degeneration of feather quality - that is, you could either eventually produce Splendids with powder-puff type of feathers, or coarse, bristly ones. The secret is to blend together both varieties and attempt to keep the size of the bird above the very small type of bird so often seen, but also keep the neater and finer feather texture.

Sometimes, this softness or weakness of the feather will cause it to distort on leaving the follicle and it will continue to develop beneath the bird's skin, resulting in the formation of a soft lump. This can be removed by a vet who would, no doubt, make an entry through the skin and remove the lump of degenerate feather tissue beneath. We believe that there is no cure for this condition once it becomes apparent, as it does appear to be caused by double yellowing - that is, breeding between birds of the softer-feathered type for too long a period, without resorting to the buff-feathered variety.

If birds of this kind *do* appear within your stud, it would be preferable if they were not used for breeding purposes, or you may end up with a possible defect being spread further throughout your stock.

FEATHER PLUCKING

This often appears to be either a nervous habit of both cock and hen Splendids and is a feature shared by many other species of bird, or it can also be carried out by bored parents. Some birds will perform this upon their young whilst still in the nest-box and occasionally a cock Splendid will only attack its young after they leave the nest. It seems to be used to drive fully-feathered young from the nest-box so that the adult pair can go to nest again and, if this occurs, removing the young from the nest-box to the floor of the cage - where the cock will continue to feed them - may be enough to stop the hen attacking the young fledglings.

Some pairs, especially if fed over-stimulating food or too much soft food, will commence this distressing feather-plucking on very young birds in the nest and we have observed that, if the parents are kept busy searching for food, less damage will be caused to the babies.

Feather-plucking seems to be hereditary in some cases but certainly not always as, if caught in time when it occurs with a pair that have not attempted to feather-pluck before, it can be stopped by altering the feeding system in many instances.

If continuous breeding is practiced with Splendids that have this habit, it is possible that a strain of birds may be formed in which this behaviour is the rule, rather than an occasional occurrence.

The feathers of the Splendids generally grow through perfectly once the young leave their parents, especially if only lightly plucked but, if the young have been seriously molested - resulting in skin-damage - the opposite is the case and the feathers rarely grow normally afterwards.

FOOD & FEEDING

Decide what quantity of seeds and other foodstuff you are likely to require throughout the breeding season and purchase enough, if possible, to last you right through, as a change in feeding partway through rearing the fledgling Splendids could result in a setback for them at the least or, at the worst, the loss of one or more from the nests.

If you should appear to be running out of seed, obtain a fresh supply as soon as possible and mix your remaining stock with an equal amount of the new. This will give your Splendids a gradual change-over and not a sudden break.

Splendids will survive and breed in spite of being fed just plain, hard canary and millet seed plus water, but it does not do the birds full justice and the results will be nowhere near the same as if they had been fed a more varied diet.

PINE NUTS   HEMP

All birds need nutrients to form the egg, bones, flesh, feathers and all the various organs of the body. They are also needed on a daily basis for the renewal of all the cells killed off or dying daily; to provide heat and energy to operate successfully; and to provide material to build the growing frame and bodies of juveniles.

SOAKED WHEAT

Examples of these nutrients are:

Carbohydrates - sugar and starch for energy and heat; *Fats and oils* are used in a similar capacity; *Protein* is needed to produce flesh, muscle, feathers, beaks and claws, together with most of the organs of the body. (There is not enough available in dry seeds such as Canary and Millet.); *Minerals*, such as Calcium, Phosphorus, Potassium, Sulphur and Manganese are all used in the formation of bone and other tissues. Salt (*Sodium Chloride*), Iron, Copper and Cobalt are used in the make-up of the blood, and Iodine, together with other minerals, for hormone production.

Vitamins, both fat- and water-soluble, are also important nutrients needed in very small quantities by the Splendids. Some of these are manufactured by the birds themselves when exposed to ultra-violet light (D3) and B12 is

-40-

manufactured by gut flora in droppings that are a few days old. Others of these groups are found in fresh, natural greenstuff but, as many vitamins are very unstable, it is best to supplement the bird's diet. Vitamins in general are needed by the Splendids in very small amounts, fed daily and, if the body receives more than it requires, the excess vitamins will only end up being excreted onto the cage floor and wasted.

Supplementary foods are now available with added vitamins formulated by the various Avian nutritionists which should take away much of the guesswork of days gone by.

When breeding in cages or inside units, keep all feeding containers in the section furthest from the position of the nest-box to minimise disturbance of the sitting hen, who may be on the nervous side and may puncture eggs whilst scrabbling around in the box.

It is imperative that the seed used for feeding your Splendids comes from a reliable source. It must be clean, uncontaminated by vermin droppings and dirt and must also be free from DDT or other harmful chemicals. If television reports are correct, DDT is still being sprayed over crops in some Third World countries to kill off locusts and other pests. It would be fatal if our birds were exposed to this chemical once again, as it caused so much harm to all kinds of birds in this country a few years ago.

Splendids in the wild go through different phases throughout the year. During the very hot, dry season the only food consists mainly of the hard, dry seeds. This will supply limited nourishment and, no doubt, the birds will fine down searching for food. With the coming of the rains, these seeds will germinate, take root and grow.

The sprouted seed undergoes great change from its original state. With alterations to the carbohydrates, the protein content increases and the seeds

-41-

become more easily assimilated by the birds. Feeding on these more nutritious substances - now including the more abundant insect life - will bring the birds from gently ticking over into really fit breeding condition and trigger off the mating and nesting instincts.

Whilst this rich food, together with soft, unripe seeds, is available on the grasses and other plants, the Splendids will be taking advantage of it and rearing their young. The young should leave the nest to still find the unripe seeds to feed on and possibly moult before the onset of lean times once more.

If possible, we must try to emulate these conditions with our feeding system. Rich, nutritious food should be made available to bring the Splendids into breeding condition and for rearing chicks. Continue feeding with lesser amounts of these foods until tailing off after the moult, then feed mainly on hard seeds for the duration of the resting period.

FEEDING DURING NON-BREEDING SEASON

The basic seed mixture we use for Splendids contains 50% Canary seed and 50% mixed Millets. Together with this we feed a mix of hemp, niger, groats and pine nuts in small quantities. Oil seeds such as hemp, niger, linseed and sunflower can be fed in small amounts only as the Splendids will, if permitted, feed off these only and so deprive themselves of the more protein-rich seeds they need. It is a bit like making children eat up their cabbage as well as the nice puddings!

Many of the seed merchants today have, with the assistance of bird nutritionists, worked out some very good seed mixtures for parrakeets in general. It will certainly be easier to purchase these rather than mix your own.

Titbits, such as small pieces of apple or berries from garden plants, are also eaten avidly by some birds. A list of berries we have fed will be added later. Grated carrot is also sought after and enjoyed by both young and old birds.

We also feed a small amount, every few days, of one of the prepared rearing soft foods to all our Splendids outside the breeding season, so there is no difficulty in getting the birds to eat it whilst breeding.

Fresh water is presented each day in open plant-pot saucers to allow bathing if required and we note that, in most cases, as soon as the water is changed it is bathed in!

Cuttlefish bone, iodine blocks and a grit mixture made up of equal parts of fine oyster shell, mineralised tonic grit and granulated charcoal, is always available to the birds all year round.

Charcoal is a must as far as we are concered. We have found it invaluable in the case of any bird with a tummy upset, as the birds readily pick it over and it absorbs the stomach juices that appear to be the cause. It is the first item to be selected from the grit pots when these are regularly replenished. It does not seem advisable to feed it *ad lib* in a separate pot, as the Splendids will eat their fill of it and leave the other grit mixture which is needed to assist in the rendering down of the seed within the bird's gizzard. Charcoal is not hard enough to do this and would itself be pulverised by the hard seeds.

Some fanciers mix cod liver oil with their seed at a ratio of 1 teaspoonful of cod liver oil to 7lbs of seeds but we do not use it, as cod liver oil can so easily go rancid and contaminate the seed if kept too long. Great care must be used if you wish to try this mixture.

Green food, such as chickweed or a little groundsel, twigs and buds from fruit trees or hazelnut bushes, young green shoots and leaves of hawthorn or May trees, together with small branches of willow, can be offered to your Splendids who will extract many hours of enjoyment picking the plants over, but make sure that all titbits - fruit included - are free from any contamination and are removed before nightfall, so that the birds go to roost on a crop full of sustaining seed rather than succulent greenery, consisting mainly of water. Little things like this can go a long way towards keeping your Splendids fit and strong during the short days and long nights of our Winter and early Spring.

As Spring approaches, we increase the daily amounts of rearing soft food and begin feeding one of the available tonic and conditioning seed mixtures. We slowly drop the oil seed mixture until, at the commencement of the breeding season, it ceases to be offered to our birds.

We have noticed that a number of breeders feed brown bread and milk to their breeding pairs, pushing this through the wire at the end of their flights on to small feeding platforms. Unfortunately, numerous wild birds soon discover this and cling to the wire, feeding from it. This could possibly lead to infection being passed, through their droppings, to the Splendids within the flight. We prefer to feed one of the ready-mixed rearing and condition foods with the other foods within the shelter or breeding unit.

If you can guarantee that the chickweed, etc., was grown in either a green-house or somewhere where there is no possibility of it being contaminated, either by chemicals or animals, then it is likely that no harm will come to your birds but, personally, we prefer to feed soaked and sprouted seed.

Unless you are very careful when feeding a variety of seeds continuously, some birds will approach the food dishes immediately they have been re-plenished, eat their fill of one or two selected seeds, and drive away all comers until they are replete. In this way, they will never eat any of the other seeds offered and will become dependent on one variety only.

This is where observation of your stock comes in as, most of the time, you will notice this happening. The obvious way of overcoming this problem would be to offer these seeds in small quantities and then only for a day or two at a time. The fact that the favourite seeds are not available at all times will ensure that your Splendids do not exist on a meagre diet of one or two selected seeds only.

COTONEASTER Horizontalis

Seeds to soak during the breeding season:

Wheat, sunflower, whole oats and canary seed.

"I think the sunflower seeds have sprouted, dear."

To soak and sprout seed, take about one cupful (depending on the number of birds you have) and cover it with water in a bucket for 24 hours. The mixture is then thoroughly washed several times and spread out in shallow trays or plates. A container with holes in the base would suffice for this. Place the container in a warm position for three or four days and keep moist until the sprouts are about 1 cm long. Wash the sprouted seed and make sure that it remains sweet-smelling and not musty before feeding it to your birds.

Great care must be taken that only fresh seed is available for the Splendids and all stale food removed daily.

Feed in this manner throughout the breeding season - small amounts of the supplementary foods to begin with until the young hatch, then increase the amount as the chicks progress in size. Reduce the amounts once more when the young Splendids leave the nest to make sure they are taking some normal seed before being separated from their parents. Millet sprays are invaluable in helping young birds graduate to hard seed.

Having a small amount of soft food available to the birds during their moult (when there is an increase of protein needed for feather production) will assist them through it, as young Splendids can be vulnerable at this time. Return to the basic seed mixture once more for birds having completed the moult until the next breeding season.

During the Autumn we offer berries from our garden, together with sweet-corn, to our Splendids. The berries ours like best are Cotoneaster, Firethorn,

Raspberries, Wild Rowan or Mountain Ash, Elder and Oregon Grape. Sketches of these and other edible fruits and plants are to be found distributed throughout this book.

It may be that many more of the berries eaten by our wild British birds could also be safely offered to our Splendids but be very careful, as two seeds - Yew and Hawthorn berries - although eaten and relished by thrushes, apparently possess kernels which are poisonous. These, while safely passing through the bodies of the thrush, would be crushed and eaten by Splendids with possible harmful effects.

We would suggest that anyone wishing to feed wild plants or berries to their Splendids consults a botanical expert before experimenting too much, as one seed, for example - the almond, is known to contain arsenic.

One particular thing which we did was much enjoyed by our young Splendids and by the pairs with eggs; we obtained some wheat and rye grass seed, after making sure it was not treated with any chemicals used to deter vermin, and soaked them together before placing them in shallow plastic dishes (previously used by butchers for meat pâté). The containers were placed in a warm position and left for about ten days, soaking occasionally. At the end of this period the green shoots were between 1" and 2" high.

All the units, trays and seedlings were thoroughly washed several times and then one was placed in each cage whilst still wet. The Splendids, both cock and hen, went down on it, almost rolling in it in their eagerness to devour it and, of course, took moisture back into the nest-boxes on their breast feathers, adding to the humidity within.

ROWAN
(Mountain Ash)
(*Sorbus aucuparia*)

FOSTERING

The use of foster parents can, in certain circumstances, be a necessity but here we are referring to using them after some unfortunate accident to the original parent birds. If you use foster parents of any species to rear another's eggs purely for increasing stock, and continue doing this for a number of generations, you are in danger of breeding a strain which may lose its own sitting and rearing instincts.

It was reported a number of years ago that, through the use of Bengalese finches purely as fosterparents for some of the rarer finches, these rarer birds appeared after a while to be unable or unwilling to rear their own young.

If you have enough pairs, it is better to discard the entire clutch from an inferior pair, if one has to foster eggs from a more valuable nest and transfer the whole clutch, rather than split them up under a number of hens. There would be no way of identifying the young from the fostered eggs if this was done. The marking of eggs is not a good practice as any material used could pass through the porous egg shell and possibly cause the death of the embryo within.

We have found it is possible to foster individual chicks which can be marked, with a vegetable dye, on one leg for identification purposes and the Splendids have, in most cases, taken to the new chick, provided that they have young about the same age. We have also found, however, that if one pair of birds abandons one of their own chicks to die, it is a complete waste of time to try and foster it out. The foster parents, also, seem to know there is something wrong with the youngster and will either also refuse to feed it and let it die, or will desert their own nest. This would appear to be nature's way of arranging for the continuation of the species, by allowing only the fittest to survive and breed. Hand-feeding could be resorted to if required but, in our experience, the chick in question rarely, if ever, survives and breeds successfully.

Turquoisines or Redrump Parrakeets can also be utilised as foster parents for Splendids but Budgerigars have been found to be unsuitable owing to the fact that baby Budgies are born hairless and the baby Splendids are covered in a hairy down from birth.

If using a Turquoisine as a foster parent it is advisable to remove all her own chicks and substitute the Splendid offspring. In this way there should be no danger of mixing the young and, perhaps, making a mistake with any young hens produced. The cocks, when moulted, would either possess the red breasts of the Splendids or the red wing bar of the Turquoisine, so that identifying the males of the different species is simple. With hens, however, it is a different matter and mistakes can and do occur.

When using Redrumps for fostering, also remove their chicks or eggs as their larger offspring could so easily trample the baby Splendids underfoot and kill them. We have had no trouble with imprinting on our young Splendids through being fostered by either Turquoisines or Redrumps if the fledglings are removed soon after leaving the nest-box and the Splendid young have all mated with their own kind during the following breeding season.

Once the chicks or eggs have been removed from a pair of Splendids and fostered, for whatever reason, we have also discovered it is useless to try and return them to the original pair after a few days, as the true parents will have become used to an empty nest-box and their desire to hatch or rear young will have evaporated.

The hen should, however, after a short while again come into lay if she is fit and healthy, and proceed to hatch and rear her next round of chicks.

Firethorn *(Pyracantha coccinea)*

GROWING UP INTO AVICULTURE

Over the years of breeding Splendids we have watched many people come into the fancy, some to stay for a lifetime and others for only a while, and we have noticed that in most cases a pattern is followed. It happened to us in much the same way - we came into aviculture, went out, then came back in once again. Generally, once the bug has bitten, the effect remains with one for life.

Pre-teen children first desire to enter the world of aviculture either through visits to zoos with schools, or in family parties. Some begin by assisting parents with their hobbies of bird-keeping, then graduate to having their own pair of birds in dad's (or mum's) birdroom. Occasionally, they are able to become the proud possessor of one of their own and spend many happy hours attending to their stock and going to Cage Bird clubs and shows. If they are lucky enough to obtain first-class stock birds, they can also breed with them, show them and eventually have their birdroom walls decorated with red tickets and rosettes, while a few will become the proud owners of other trophies, and all of them will make lifelong friends along the way.

As they grow older, school work and examinations have to take priority over their hobby of aviculture and their stock is either taken over by others within the family group or sold, and the treasured birdroom becomes a garden shed once more. The late teen years are taken up with job training or further study and the opposite sex grows more interesting and important with each passing year.

By the time they reach their early thirties, they will probably have married, had a family, settled down in a job and may have their own homes and gardens. The opportunity then arises once more to pursue their bird-keeping hobby. The garden can now be laid out to their own family requirements - a hard-standing area for the family washing-line, with a play area for the children nearby if desired; a small lawn, with an aviary or birdroom in the background, framed by a blaze of colour in the nearby flower beds. A delight to behold and an interest to occupy them for many years if not for their entire lives. Kept in proportion, it will prove to be a combined interest for both husband and wife to enjoy, together with the social life to be found by joining a local club and taking an active part in the activities afforded by it.

GREENHOUSES

These are unsuitable for using as a birdroom or shelter for Splendids as the extremes in temperature between day and night during the summer and winter months would be too great. The problem of security for the birds with the vents open would entail virtually enclosing the openings with wire mesh and, unless the whole was enclosed likewise, the entire stud could be lost in the event of accidental breakage of the glass walls.

Unless one goes to great expense in installing a heating system to even out the vast temperature range that would be likely, losses would occur among the enclosed birds. It would be far cheaper to provide a wooden hut for use as a birdroom, than to provide a system of this kind.

All birds like to retreat into a corner or cover of some kind to escape from danger, either real or imagined, and being surrounded by glass would deny them this facility.

Breeding cages generally consist of five sides being made of plywood or a similar material, with only the front having a wire mesh construction. The condensation forming on the large expanse of glass would also greatly increase the humidity within the structure - this would certainly not suit the Splendids, which are essentially birds from a dry, desert area.

GREGARIOUSNESS

The only time that Splendids could be considered gregarious is in the Autumn and Winter, when they can be observed feeding in the wild in small family parties. They do not congregate in large flocks but, whether this is due to a scarcity of them locally or, as it would appear to be, their desire to remain in separate groups, has yet to be decided upon.

In captivity we have found that they will pair for life but will also accept another mate if one of the pair should meet with an unfortunate death.

Should this happen, we introduce another partner after any nest of chicks the survivor was rearing has become independent.

If you wish to pair a single cock Splendid with two hens in the same season, we have found the best time to remove the cock is when the young of the first hen are about a fortnight old, and place him in another birdroom so that the pair cannot hear each other calling.

Do not introduce another hen to the cock for another couple of weeks after separating and it will then be possible that they will accept each other and produce full eggs.

It has apparently been tried to breed with one cock running with two or three hens, but with what success we do not know. We do not recommend anyone trying this because, if a dominant hen was among the group the other two would not last long. The same would apply if two or more cock Splendids were in the same enclosure for breeding purposes. Try these various methods of breeding if you must, but beware!

GUESSWORK

When attending to any form of livestock, there is not too much room for guesswork. It is far better for the Splendids - and for you - if you ask as many questions as you wish of other fanciers, to get their opinions. Remember that almost any book or answer to a question is only one person's opinion and there will be many answers to the same question. None will be identical, but most will be generally the same. We do not believe there is a perfect solution to any aspect of keeping, feeding and breeding Splendids or any other species, but what works for one person does not necessarily work for everyone.

You will find that Splendids are as individual as we are and it is a question of travelling along a reasonably-defined road to attend to their needs but - and this is the beauty of it - there is room for intelligent experimentation in an attempt to discover the most beneficial way of proceeding for your Splendids and yourselves.

HEATING

Splendids are perfectly hardy birds and, in general, need no heated quarters to keep them healthy. They can withstand cold but damp and draughty conditions will harm them. If one is breeding in outside aviaries, so long as the birds are shut into a snug shelter during the cold nights and foggy weather, and you make sure that they go to bed in a dry condition, they should keep reasonably fit but, at the first signs of any sickness, then the birds should be taken into warmer conditions.

The Splendids should not be allowed access to a nest-box in an outside exposed situation until the end of April or early May under these aviary breeding conditions, although some years - especially if the late winter is very mild - it will prove to be a hard task to keep the pairs from breeding.

Breeding within a birdroom is a different matter, however. The Splendids, being insulated from the worst rigours of winter weather, will come into breeding condition that much earlier and, with heat being available to them, they can be provided with nest-boxes in February.

Various methods of heating have been used at times for birdrooms, ranging from paraffin-oil greenhouse heaters to gas and electricity.

If one uses paraffin heaters, you must use one that has been especially constructed for the purpose and the operating instructions must be faithfully adhered to, regarding the correct type of fuel and condition of the wicks. It is imperative that the wick is correctly cleaned and trimmed, to obtain an even, blue flame. In the past, many accidents have occurred in birdrooms owing to these instructions not being strictly followed, resulting in malfunction of the heaters which have given off choking smoke and covered everything in the birdroom in a black, greasy film, often with tragic results. With modern and up-to-date oil heaters there is less likelihood of this happening if operating instructions are followed at all times.

Remember, however, that an amazing amount of water is released into the air with the burning of every gallon of paraffin oil, therefore the room must be very well-ventilated and be prepared to mop up a lot of water from condensation off windows and walls.

A mobile, propane gas heater could also be used but would have to be treated with caution. Both the above forms of heating use oxygen for combustion and, unless the birdroom is very well-ventilated, would very quickly use up all of this valuable and essential component of the air. This could result in the suffocation of your birds. Propane gas also releases plenty of water into the air, so condensation could again be a problem, especially if any electricity is used in the birdroom for lighting or heating, etc.

Electricity is also used for heating in its various forms; convectors, bar-heaters, panels, tubular or fan heaters. One note of caution, however, with all forms of heating involving a flame or exposed radiation heating element. Small feathers, feather-dust and seed husks are present in all birdrooms and, if any of these materials settled on these hot surfaces, a fire could develop with disastrous results.

In our birdrooms we have tubular heaters. These are controlled by thermo-stats, which we consider to be the safest method. The electricity is switched off until we have the Splendids paired and set up in mid-February, at which time we energise the system. The heating is set to come on when the birdroom temperature drops below 40°F, (around 5°C), so it usually is only required on rare occasions for short periods. This temperature prevents the water in the pots from freezing and makes it more pleasant for the birds, and for us when attending to them.

We have discovered that our non-breeding hens, having only this gentle heat available to them, are able to have access to the outside flights during the day with no ill effects. If the temperature were held much higher, then - apart from the cost - we might be making our Splendids too soft and they could easily become chilled if allowed into the outside flights. It could also induce them to go into a premature moult, due to the wildly fluctuating temperatures.

It is never advisable to return a bird that has been sick and treated in a hospital cage (and, therefore, high temperatures) into a cold aviary until it has been completely acclimatised and this often means keeping the birds inside until Spring. The same comments apply if one intends showing one's Splendids during the cold winter months. If they have been inside a heated hall for a couple of days, it would be fatal to return them, straight into an exposed, outside aviary until properly acclimatised once more. This would mean subjecting the birds to a slowly-reducing temperature range, perhaps over several weeks, according to the severity of the weather, until they were used to the shelter being unheated.

Splendids are small creatures and are, therefore, unable to keep themselves warm over an extended period, after being kept in high temperatures and then kept in an environment like our British winter.

It would be possible to heat a building used for breeding only to a much higher temperature if you wish, or can afford it, and you would then be able to breed the birds throughout the entire year, but any young produced, or older moulting pairs, would be unable to have access to outside flights until the Summer-time. Anyone buying birds from such a source should, of necessity, be made aware of the birds' normal environment so that they would not place them into unheated quarters until late Spring, at least.

HAWKS

The activities of hawks of various kinds can, on occasions, cause havoc within aviaries containing young or mature Splendid Grass Parrakeets.

It is well-known that some Splendids appear to possess thin skulls and can come to grief during their mad panic, which sends them crashing into the roof or walls of their aviaries when approached by a hawk.

The mad scramble will be followed by an eerie, quiet period for both Splendids and wild birds, during which all the living birds will be frozen into immobility for a while. We have occasionally found one or two Splendids on their backs with broken necks after such a commotion.

If the aviary roofs are covered with opaque plastic sheets, this will prevent the hawks from seeing the Splendids below and *vice versa*. We have discovered that a layer of dark-green, small mesh, plastic horticultural netting hung onto the sides of the aviary helps prevent any attack to those areas by the hawks. It does not look very pretty but it achieves the desired effect of protecting the Splendids.

Occasionally large, hot-air balloons pass over our property and we have noticed a similar eerie silence descend upon the birds. We then see them craning their necks and peering up into the sky in an enquiring fashion. (One can almost hear them asking their companions, "Whassat?")

HOMING SPLENDIDS

Flocks of homing Budgerigars are to be found in many places and, as these birds are normally gregarious and form large groups in the wild, it works quite well when they are kept in semi-captivity.

As Splendids generally form small family groups, we do not think one could use the same system for them. However, as these birds form a very strong pair-bond, in common with many species of softbills and some hardbills, the cock bird could possibly be given limited liberty when the young birds are hatched and needing a varied diet. Some breeders of foreign softbills apparently open the aviary door and allow the cocks to forage for live food in the surrounding area. Splendids spend a lot of time on the floor, picking over various objects, and it is possible that they could benefit from having their freedom for short periods.

One would have to be very brave to attempt this when breeding Splendids and you would have to have an area free from cats or hawks of any kind, but it would be a wonderful picture to see a cock Splendid, in his full regalia, foraging in the garden for titbits to delight the palate of his mate and their babies.

The parent birds will need to be secured once more before the young Splendids leave the nest-box, or losses will occur during the first few days among the juveniles whilst they are learning to fly. Later the whole family group may also decide to go "walk-about" and leave the vicinity of their nesting site.

HANDLING YOUR SPLENDIDS

In general, the more chicks are handled in the nest, the steadier and more tame they become, but this applies only if the adult pair are amenable enough to allow you to do this. Some pairs would desert the young if they were interfered with very much, whilst others would remain in the open nest-box whilst their young were being rung, or handled for any other purpose.

Attending to any nest-box duties is best done only when you are relaxed and contented with what you are attempting. If these activities - handling the chicks for ringing, etc. - are carried out whilst you are upset or edgy, it is very likely that your mood will be picked up by the birds themselves, who may (and often do) become fractious and edgy themselves, causing problems of all kinds and, perhaps, resulting in escapes or injuries.

When relaxed you will notice that this also will be transmitted to the birds, which will become more confident and approachable in many cases.

All movements towards the birds should be done in a slow, deliberate manner, which will do much to retain their confidence, as you will find that quick movements towards almost any Splendid will cause them to react in a like manner and try to escape from your hands.

Don't take too many liberties with any of your Splendids until you know the temperament of each pair, or even single birds. They are all individuals, as we are, and even the most placid ones among them can have their off-days when they are easily upset and do not possess their usual tranquility.

The Splendid is generally a friendly little bird who will come to the front of its cage or aviary when the owners approach and greet them with a delightful little call, almost enquiring "What have you brought for me on this visit?"

Quite often, however, when the owner visits with a companion - if the birds only rarely receive visits from strangers - they will disappear, either into the shelter or a nest-box if one is available.

To obtain really tame birds, however, one must handle them whilst very young and still in the nest, providing the parent Splendids are amenable and willing for you to do this. You must get to know your birds.

If the nest-boxes are opened at regular times and the parent birds are presented with a favourite titbit - perhaps a slice of sweet apple or a short length of millet spray - the parents will be too busy investigating their treasure to be really concerned with you looking at and handling the young fledglings. If the parents show any signs of agitation, then it is best to close the nest-box and leave well alone.

Some parent birds would desert the young if they were interfered with too much but luckily this is the exception rather than the rule. We have found others who refused to leave and remained within the open nest-box all the while their young were being rung or handled for any other purpose. We, however, like our Splendids to be a little cautious so that, although they will nearly all come to the wire when we approach the aviary, they will fly away from, rather than towards us, when we actually enter their enclosures. This, we feel, helps to prevent us from either stepping on the birds around our feet on the aviary floor, or the Splendids escaping past us when we enter through the doors.

When a Splendid needs to be caught up by hand, it is first advisable to coax it into as small a compartment as possible to prevent a prolonged chase. Unless the bird can be caught almost immediately, it will only cause it and yourself distress and frustration. Continued harrassment will make the Splendid try harder to escape and it could easily do itself an injury - the last thing anyone would wish to do.

Obviously, for a beginner to attempt this manoeuvre with both human and bird being nervous of each other, it will be more fraught with stress than for an experienced aviculturist, but we all need to learn. It is very often best for a beginner to learn the technique of catching his or her birds by first practising with a very young bird or a tame adult, neither of which would be caused excessive stress by their owner's actions.

When a cupped hand is placed into the cage the Splendid may at first panic and fly to each end, but will shortly land in one corner. If you are right-handed, allow the bird to land in the left-hand front corner and you should be able to cover it with your hand. Left-handed people should wait for it to use the right-hand corner. Should the bird repeatedly escape you after three or four attempts, leave it to settle down and recover before repeating your actions.

If the Splendid can be induced to enter a show-cage fitted to the end of your units or compartments, however, there will be no need for the above actions, as you would be able to apprehend the bird at your first attempt.

One way to restrain a bird securely is to hold it on its back in your palm and, gently placing forefinger and thumb each side of its head, grasp the jawbone, thus preventing the beak from turning and biting you. Fold your other three fingers across its chest and abdomen and allow it to grip your little finger with its feet.

HOSPITAL CAGES

Anyone keeping or breeding livestock will find at some time or another that one or more of their charges will fall sick and need treatment of some kind. Generally, if noticed as soon as it is off-colour, the bird can be caught up and caged on its own with a little warmth and, left to its own devices, it will recover and soon be back in the aviary with its fellows.

The most effective form of treatment for a sick bird is heat and this can be provided either by heating the bird's own cage or by providing a specially-constructed hospital cage.

A simple method of supplying heat to a bird that is a little off-colour is by the use of a portable heater, as used by pig and poultry breeders. This consists of an aluminium reflector on an extension lead, with a porcelain screw-type lamp holder within. Non-shatter, infra-red lamps are available for use with these reflectors, ranging from 50w to 250w if required. We use a 150w emitter connected to a dimmer switch which enables us to have much greater control over the amount of heat used.

This lamp can be hung onto the cage front of any of our breeding compartments and facing a perch. This causes no stress to the inhabitant - perhaps a hen noticed to be having difficulty in passing an egg - who would otherwise have to be caught up and placed into a hospital cage. This, however, may have to be accomplished as a last resort.

As soon as the lamp is switched on it will begin to emit heat but not light and it is surprising how swiftly a distressed bird will notice this and position itself up tight to the cage front, on the perch nearest the lamp. The beauty of this system is that the bird can move away from the lamp if it becomes overheated or no longer needs the warmth or can, likewise, approach the lamp when extra warmth is required.

This lamp is also used by us after a Splendid has been ill enough to be placed in a hospital cage. It can be utilised as a half-way measure between hospitalisation and being returned to an open flight.

The hospital cage generally consists of a box made or wood or metal, with a wire and glass panel front and an entry door at one end. These can be obtained in various sizes for large or small birds and are heated either by a small tubular heater, thermostatically-controlled, or by the use of two electric lightbulbs situated beneath the metal cage floor. These two bulbs are separately switched to provide a high temperature quickly by the use of both bulbs at first, then sustaining a reasonable temperature by switching one off. We have found that, by using one 100w bulb and one 60w, we can provide the temperatures required. A thermometer placed inside the cage shows us what the temperature is within.

When the bird is first placed in the hospital cage using two bulbs, the unit must not be left unattended until a temperature of around 75°-80°F is reached, at which time one bulb must be switched off. Failure to switch off one lamp could easily cause the cage interior to become unbearably hot, resulting in the premature death of your Splendid.

It is most unwise, in our opinion, to keep a hospital cage containing a sick bird in the birdroom with your healthy stock, as this could result in more of your Splendids becoming infected. It is preferable if it can be situated in a separate building away from other birds. In an emergency a heat source for a sick bird can be made from a low-power electric lightbulb, on a "wander-lead", being placed under a large biscuit tin within a cage. A small degree of temperature regulation may be obtained by raising or lowering the biscuit tin above the lamp, but care must be taken to ensure the temperature of the tin does not overheat and cause a fire or other damage.

In a birdroom or aviary shelter where no electricity is available, a small oil heater of the covered type that is used beneath cars during frosty weather may well be utilised but, if so, make sure that the wick is cleaned and trimmed correctly to avoid the hazard of smoke and, perhaps, fire. Even a gentle heat is comfort for a sick bird and is better than no heat at all. When a Splendid has been so ill that it has needed to be confined in a hospital cage with continuous heat, do not be too eager to return it to the environment of an exposed aviary.

It is advisable to first lower the temperature of the hospital cage by degrees, until the bird has become acclimatised to being in unheated surroundings, before introducing it once more to a few of its fellows We are all aware that, if any of us is under the weather, we prefer to make our own way slowly back into the busy and crowded world, rather than be hurled headlong into it. Select a mild day for the bird's eventual release into the outside world and watch carefully that the recovered Splendid repairs to its shelter for food and, for the first few days, shut it in at night.

INBREEDING AND LINE BREEDING

This is a subject over which discussion has waxed long and loud. On the one side, people desire completely unrelated stock whilst, on the other, anyone wishing to breed top-class, show-winning stock of all breeds, goes in for matings as close as mother/son and father/daughter. If anyone embraces a system of breeding unrelated Splendids, then the gene-pool within each cock and hen will consist of a vast number of differing components, each of which would be responsible for a particular feature in their young's make-up. The random selection and coming together of two particles within the egg - we shall call them genes for ease of identification - one each from the cock and the hen, will determine each feature of the young Splendid's body, from the colour of its eye to the length and sharpness of its toenails.

Within this vast pool, passed down and added to by all its ancestors, matings of this kind will produce a stud of Splendids that has no uniformity of any kind. The chances of a new mutation occurring within a stud of this kind would also be very remote, as many of these are either sex-linked or recessive, so the new factor would become so diluted through unrelated matings that it would rarely surface and produce a Splendid showing the new feature.

However, this type of breeding is admirable for anyone breeding Splendids purely for the purpose of producing birds to satisfy their own requirements and maybe selling their surplus to others of a like mind. At the time of writing, there is no recognised show type or standard to aim for and very little serious showing of Splendids is undertaken.

Many birds bred in this manner are of the so-called "wild" type and tend to be of all shapes, sizes and depths of colour.

Inbreeding, or the breeding of related stock, can also fall into various groups, e.g. "Line breeding" where all the birds of one group would be bred from, say, one outstanding cock paired to two or three good hens and any promising female paired back to the cock; also young cocks back to related females.

This type of breeding can be done with stock for which there is a recognised show standard and the master cock is a top winner at shows. It would be hoped that pairings of this kind would result in the smaller gene-pool available being more likely to form a desirable combination and produce a specimen which would be approaching the standard of the master cock, or possibly surpass it.

When a young cock is bred which excels the master cock he, in turn, becomes the master and is paired with a further two or three good hens, and so on. A similar breeding programme can also be followed to breed excellent hens.

Sometimes this system is used with birds that possess one or two outstanding features and these particular attributes would become a dominant feature within the gene-pool. One of the birds from this line could then be used as an out-cross and bred with a prize-winning show specimen which needs the exaggerated feature to, perhaps, bring its young to perfection.

This is how it should work in theory and it does produce a few specimens, but it also produces many young that do not approach show standards at all, as the "coming-together" of the genes to produce the good visual, or otherwise, show features is purely a random event. Obviously, the more in-bred the birds become, the smaller the gene-pool and the likelihood of young birds now being bred which approach the standard of their parents, becomes higher.

This is why, when some breeding establishments are visited, the birds appear to be like "peas from the same pod". When birds are purchased from a stud that practices in-breeding or line-breeding, one has to purchase any out-cross that may be desired, either from the original breeder or from the breeders of similarly-bred stock.

A few words of warning, however, if serious in-breeding is is contemplated - you must select the best stock available to breed with each season and discard all others. Records must be carefully kept and, should any set of pairs produce rubbish, then the lines of each may be suspect and should not be used in the main breeding programme until test-mated and proved to be beneficial. Remember, in-breeding fixes all visual and hidden characteristics and it has been known on occasions that some particular visual attributes also carry with them very undesirable hidden ones, as can be seen from some of the defects in various types of show animals today.

Colour mutations are generally found more in closely-inbred families or lines, as the gene-pool is that much reduced and the young carrying the recessive genes are more likely to be bred with close relatives carrying like attributes.

Some of these recessive genes, when combined, can prove fatal to the offspring. We have heard that the pairing together of visually Blue Splendids can sometimes cause this effect but at the time of writing this book we have not yet experienced this ourselves. For this reason the production of Blue Splendids is preferably obtained from the pairing together of one visually Blue Splendid to a split Blue bird. So-called "lethal" genes were also blamed many years ago, among the Budgerigar fanciers, for the losses experienced when trying to breed the rare Violet variety. It would appear that single-factor young, (when they were bred from a visual Violet and a normal-coloured bird which was carrying the recessive Violet factor, i.e. normal split to Violet) would mostly survive but that double-factor young (bred from two visual Violets) seldom did.

ILLNESS & INJURIES

The first thing we notice about an ailing bird is the eye. Instead of a bright, wide-open and shining bead, we are confronted with a partly-closed and almost pain-glazed orb. This is a condition hard to explain but instantly recognisable by almost every fancier.

Watch the bird for a short while to ascertain whether it is distressed because of bullying by any other member of the group and, if so, remove the offending bird to another location.

If this is not the case, catch up and examine the Splendid for any sign of obvious injury. One fairly common occurrence is for a bird - in a panic over some possibly trivial thing - to crash headlong into the side of the aviary or cage, when one or more of its wing feathers may pass through the wire and become fractured. The bird will feel uncomfortable over this condition, which may not show up until it is caught and examined. The gentle withdrawal of the broken feather stub or stubs will alleviate the condition and the Splendid should soon recover.

Any major injury requiring the services of the veterinary surgeon should be immediately attended to. If no injury can be found, isolate the bird immediately from its fellows and place into a cage on its own. A bird that is sickening will progress from this condition to standing on the perch with both feet down, feathers all fluffed out to retain body heat and head tucked back under the feathers of its shoulder. A healthy bird will also occasionally assume this position but will generally elevate one leg up into its tummy feathers.

If the bird becomes really distressed and ill, it will be discovered huddled on the floor of the cage in a similar position - on two feet - and quite often in a corner. Generally, birds and animals, if sick, will attempt to hide themselves away and suffer in silence.

Your local vet, specialising in birds and animals, should be consulted early on in the development of any illness, as some of the diseases which show only mild symptoms could develop into serious conditions. If an ailing Splendid can receive early professional medication, in most cases it will survive and completely recover but, if a vet is only consulted after all home-made treatments have failed, it may be too late to save the bird.

All healthy Splendids regurgitate seed to feed each other or their young, but a bird on its own on a perch who consistently brings up seed from its crop and then shakes its head violently, scattering the partly-digested food in all directions, needs attention as soon as possible to settle its stomach, at least.

Occasionally a Splendid will be noticed standing on the perch stretching, face-upwards, and commencing to twirl its head so violently that it will overbalance and fall from the perch. This action can be caused by the bird striking its head and damaging its skull or brain, a condition that could possibly right itself if the bird was isolated for a few days. However, it could also be a symptom of a tumour, among other things, so we would always recommend obtaining professional advice if in any doubt.

INVOLVEMENT OF FAMILIES

The pleasurable hobby of breeding Splendid Grass Parrakeets can be given an added dimension if the whole family can be involved in it. Apart from the distribution of labour attending to the stock, it will mean more time for all to enjoy the company of the birds and the family can be engaged together visiting other fanciers to obtain replacement or outcrosses.

We have often noticed at shows one interested member of the family thoroughly enjoying the occasion while others are either sitting in the car or standing dejectedly in one corner of the hall, trying to attract the attention of the lone fancier to drag him or her away.

When a spouse becomes a true partner in the breeding of Splendids or any other stock, it immediately becomes obvious. No longer is he or she just the tea-maker for visitors and kept on the sidelines during "birdie" conversations with other fanciers. Also, if husband and wife are both involved in the hobby, it can go a long way towards preventing any build-up of resentment such as "He is spending all his time and money on his birds and neglecting us", etc.

We enjoy visiting other fanciers and have them visit us and notice immediately those families where the children have been actively brought up with birds and those who have not. Youngsters of all species need to let off a bit of steam, or life would become very dull for them, but the children involved with the family birds and their breeding activities know that there is a time and place for everything. Inside a birdroom is not the place to go crashing about.

We have discovered over the years the pleasure that is afforded to youngsters by the possession of even a single pair of birds of their very own. They begin to realise the responsibility in having to care for their charges - feeding, cleaning and the general husbandry involved. The delight shown by them on the appearance of their very first eggs of the season and the minute attention to detail that is often shown by children surprises many of we adults who live fairly busy lives.

It enables them to stretch their imagination towards devising many interesting little pieces of equipment for use with their birds and, because their minds are uncluttered by trained lines of thought in any sphere, they are able to view many things from a different aspect to an adult.

Seed

Dandelion
(Taraxacum officinale)

JARGON

In common with nearly all specialist clubs or societies, bird-keeping has its own language which can be completely unintelligible to the rest of the world unfortunate enough not to share our hobby. In this section we will endeavour to explain some of these expressions for newcomers to our ranks. These are the usual expressions used by breeders of all parrot-like species.

Addled Egg - an egg in which the chick has commenced to form but, for one reason or another, has died.

Barhead (Budgerigar) - a juvenile bird which has yet to enter its first moult and develop a clear forehead.

Benched - a term used when showing birds. It means literally that the bird is in a showcage being judged along with its peers.

Blood Quill - a newly-emerging feather, generally one of the large flight or tail feathers which has a thick, blood-filled quill as it develops.

Clear Egg - an unfertilised egg.

Closed Ring - a metal ring generally constructed of a light metal such as aluminium, made in numerous sizes to fit most birds and slipped over the bird's foot onto its leg during the first week or so of its life. If the correct-sized ring for the species is used, it may only be removed by cutting it through.

Crop Milk - a milky secretion regurgitated by most parrot-like and a few other hens. It is usually produced by the birds and fed to very young hatchlings which would be unable to assimilate the partially-digested seed or other foods which would be fed to older chicks. It could possibly be compared to the colostrum, or first milk, secreted by mammals after they have given birth.

Double-Yellowing - the pairing together of two birds, each of which excels in very fine and soft feather quality.

Double-Buffing - as above, but in this case each bird would possess large and coarse feathering.

Double Factor - the offspring produced by two birds each possessing the same colour or other attribute.

Duff cock or hen - a bird with which the owner has been unable to breed.

Dirty Feeder - A parent bird which feeds its young in such a messy fashion that it leaves the youngster with its beak, face and possibly nostrils encased in a crust of solidified food.

[With a parent bird of this kind care must be taken to ensure the interior of the upper mandible of the young birds is kept clean. This can be achieved by gently prising loose any semi-hardened food with an object such as a wooden toothpick, otherwise an undershot beak may ensue.]

Egg-Bound - a hen found in a distressed condition through being unable to expel the egg.

Fine Down - to develop from being too fat and ungainly to becoming slim, alert and in an appropriate breeding condition.

Follicle - a small depression on the bird's skin which contains the feather roots and from which the feathers emerge.

Flighted (Canary) - Bird which has undergone a complete moult.

Unflighted - young, unmoulted bird.

Going Light - a bird of any age which suddenly loses all the flesh from its bones for no apparent reason. The breastbone takes on the feel and appearance of the keel of an upturned boat.

Hard Bills - birds which live almost entirely on seeds or plant material.

Internal Layer - a hen which takes on the appearance of a laying hen and goes through all the stages of laying but, instead of producing eggs, reabsorbs the embryo before producing the hard, protective calcium shell and expelling it.

In the Cards - a term used when exhibiting birds which refers to any exhibit achieving a position, within any class, that merits a place card.

Master Cock or Hen - An adult bird of either sex being paired to two or three different mates during a serious breeding programme, in an attempt to upgrade stock. This system is used in line breeding for quality and to fix desirable attributes.

Maiden Hen - a hen of any age that has remained unmated.

On the Sticks - Juveniles which have left the nest and become independent from their parents are referred to as being "out on the sticks".

Parrot-like - any bird, with the exception of the birds of prey, which possesses the short, curved beak typical of the Parrot family.

Parrot - Members of the above family which, in general, possess a short, angular tail.

Parrakeet - Parrot-like birds, in general, which possess a long, pointed tail.

Pin Feathers - Short, spiky, blood-filled and immature feathers appearing generally on head or neck of birds during the moulting process.

Runt or **Rinnik** - the last and smallest bird hatched and reared from any clutch of eggs. Generally completely formed and able to reproduce. Runts are used in the breeding of some miniature strains of animals.

Runner - any bird unable to fly, owing to the onset of a disease called French Moult. This distressing complaint results in the atrophy of the blood quills of both tail and flight feathers. These quills rot and snap off, leaving short stubs still attached to the unfortunate bird. The cause and cure for this is still not fully understood and, in our opinion, breeding with birds so affected is not to be recommended.

Single Factor - birds bred with only one parent possessing an unusual colour or other attribute and the other being a normal of that particular species.

Soft Moult - this condition is experienced when a bird has an incomplete and lengthy moult, resulting in odd feathers being dropped and replaced at any time, instead of a swift, natural change of plumage.

Soft Bill - birds that feed mainly or exclusively on insects and other live food in the wild.

Soft food - a group of preparatory or home-made mixtures, made up of both animal and vegetable matter with a cereal base. These can be obtained in various grades and proportions, which make them admirable for the feeding of Softbills when they can be fed together with live food such as maggots, meal and buffalo worms and locusts, to name but a few. Others of a different recipe can be used as a supplement to be fed to hard bills and parrot-like birds during the breeding season, especially when rearing their young.

Split Ring - a flat ring made from a hard plastic which is not joined together at one point. With the use of a special narrow, scoop-shaped tool, the ring can be enlarged enough to fit over the bird's leg at any age and, with the removal of the expanding tool, the ring will return to its original size and fit snugly to the leg. These rings may be obtained in various colours and stamped with identifying numbers or letters and are in varying sizes to fit different species.

Split Blue, etc. - Many of the different colours and types of birds are produced through the action of a recessive gene. For example, to produce a Blue Splendid, one would either have to pair together two Blue parents, one Blue parent and a split Blue parent, or two split Blue parents. The split Blue Splendid would be a visibly normal-coloured bird but would be carrying a hidden, recessive gene, perhaps obtained by its parents being one normal Splendid and one Blue bird. All of the offspring from this particular pairing would be visual normal but split to Blue and would be capable of producing

Blue young if paired back to a visual Blue or split Blue mate. The proportion of visual Blue youngsters would depend on the type of pairing.

Strain - A person may be said to have a strain when they have been breeding from a number of originally unrelated birds for a number of years and eventually, by inbreeding or line breeding, have obtained a collection of birds which all possess similar qualities. These should be capable of being reproduced among each other and the birds capable of transferring their good points to another strain by selective breeding.

Stud - the entire collection of any person, which may consist of any amount of different strains.

Type & Deportment - This term is almost impossible to describe and is much used among the showing fraternities. Any bird which possesses type is the one which generally begets admiration even from people who know nothing about birds or livestock of any kind. It is the one which draws the eye at any show or in any birdroom. It does not necessarily need to be a specimen which possesses an excess of the individual features by which breeders of exhibition stock set so much store. A Splendid possessing type will stand proudly and fearlessly before you, subjecting you to the same scrutiny as it is receiving, and treat you almost as an equal. It will deport itself like a guardsman - standing erect and holding its wings and tail evenly and in line with its body - not slouching across the perch in an untidy fashion. Type and deportment are qualities you can breed into a stud but, if they are not present in any particular specimen, it is virtually impossible for it to acquire them by training.

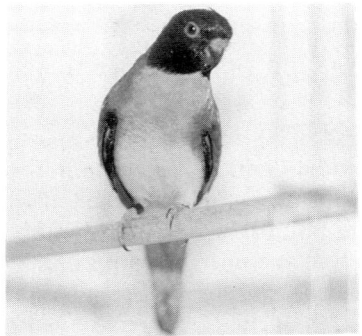

Undershot beak - a condition found among parrot-like birds where the underbeak has grown out beyond the level of the long upper mandible. The bird will still be able to feed but it will look unsightly and the lower beak, which grows quite rapidly, will need regular clipping back. This condition can also be caused by a dirty feeder parent, where the hardened food has stuck to the inside of the upper mandible of the chick, preventing the lower one from locating correctly within it. This will depress the lower beak, which will soon protrude out past the curved point of the upper, as it is no longer being worn down. In our experience, it is rare for the condition, once established, to correct itself.

When attending a bird Show, birds may be classed as:

VHC - signifying that the exhibit is Very Highly Commended.

HC - signifying Highly Commended

WC - signifying Wrongly Classed, which probably means that the bird has been entered for a competition in a section or class containing a different species or type from the bird itself.

JUVENILES (Treatment of)

When young Splendids first leave the nest they will fly headlong into the end of their enclosures until they learn to control their wing and tail movements to alter their course and to stop. This is generally accomplished within a few days but, as they usually leave the nest at intervals and not all at once, the later fledglings will crash around into all and sundry and, no doubt, cause blind panic among their more advanced nest companions.

This is when one must be very careful that there are no jagged pieces of metal, wire or small twigs around on which the immature birds could injure themselves. Also, you should ensure that the sides and ends of the aviaries are made more visible by the addition of sprigs of soft, evergreen plants or you could even use plastic horticultural netting. These precautions help to prevent any injuries, should the inmates think they have nothing to limit their flight.

For the next couple of weeks they will still beg food from their parents and the hen will often commence laying her next clutch of eggs, leaving the cock Splendid to complete the rearing alone. The fledglings will soon begin chewing on everything in sight to discover whether or not it is edible and, as the days go by, they will provide themselves with more food and will need less from their parents. This is the period during which the young birds will attempt to eat almost anything put before them so, if you have been experiencing difficulty in enticing the parents to feed on soft food, for example, now would be the time to add it to the youngsters' diet. We find a little blue Maw seed added to the soft food will tempt most of our young Splendids to pick at the mixture, thereby getting a taste and - generally finding it to their liking - they will proceed to eat it. It is always advisable to introduce a soft food of some kind to your Splendids, as it is a perfect medium in which to blend any medication which may subsequently be necessary during the bird's lifetime.

On occasions a fledgling cock will leave the nest-box with red feathers over a portion or the whole of its breast. When this occurs, the adult cock may either refuse to feed it or even physically attack it. Should this happen you may have to resort to hand-rearing for a short while. We have found that a plastic hypodermic syringe, minus the needle, is invaluable at this time. A small amount of wet, but not sloppy, soft food can be placed in the instrument and, by gently squeezing the plunger, the extruding food can be offered to the bird. It will be sampled tentatively at first but will soon be avidly devoured. We have only used this method as supplementary feeding three or four times a day, as we have noticed that, if the unfortunate bird is housed with one or two older and weaned young Splendids, it will then emulate them and soon begin to feed off the soaked seed and other goodies on offer.

The young birds may be left with the parents, even if the hen recommences sitting, for about a month after leaving the nest, so long as they are not being attacked by either parent. They should be removed if any of them re-enters the nest-box and causes distress to the sitting hen. Normally, neither of these situations occur but be aware that it may happen. In any event, the young should be removed from the parents before the next round of chicks are due to hatch.

We like to place our weaned Splendids in holding cages or aviaries with other groups of juveniles and leave them together until the onset of the moult, when they are then split up into separate groups according to sex. This, we find, prevents any undesirable pair-bonding and subsequent fighting to secure territory or mates.

KEEPING TO A SYSTEM

Before you begin to acquire and keep Splendids, visit other fanciers of a like mind and take note of their methods of caring for their stock. All of us, you will find, follow a similar pattern but with small variations - perhaps over seed mixtures or extras being fed. Times for attending to the birds may be different, or the amount of time spent in the birdroom, etc.

Decide on a system as near as possible to that used by the person from whom you purchased your Splendids but do not necessarily be too slavish about it. One of the attractions in aviculture is the fact that we may adopt our own pattern for looking after our birds within fairly broad limits.

Do not chop and change with the basic seed mixtures once you have established your birds, but it is possible to experiment with the feeding of extra seeds or berries as they come into season.

When the adult pairs have young in the nest, keep to a particular pattern of feeding until the young become independent. In this way they should suffer no setbacks or losses. This is why we advocate purchasing enough seed to last you from the start to the finish of the breeding season. During the breeding season we visit our stock in the mornings to check on everything, change the water and renew the dishes of soft food. In the evening we repeat the process and then blow off any seed-husks and replenish any seed or grit pots requiring it. At this time we also attend to any ringing required or transfer any young Splendids ready to be moved.

We find that, by keeping to a routine, the birds begin to show signs of excitement on our approach and come to the wire to greet us. This turns out to be only cupboard-love, however, for they are certainly far more interested in the titbits of food we place before them than they are with our presence.

KERATIN

This is a member of a group of proteins to be found in skin, hair, nails and feathers, among other things. Perhaps it is because some Splendids suffer from a lack of protein in their diet that they play with and chew on the quill of any large feather found on the floor of their cage and it may have some bearing on the distressing habit of feather-plucking practiced by some birds.

KNOWLEDGE

No matter how old one becomes or how long you have been engaged with a hobby, some new, often exciting, discovery appears. Perhaps you may become interested in genetics, for example, and how to improve your stud if it is lacking in a particular characteristic, or how to increase your stock of a particular mutant colour.

On the other hand, the field of avian dietetics can be of great interest to some people who would love to provide those little extras for their Splendids. The study of wild birds and their various feeding habits may give you ideas for providing a more varied diet during the different seasons of the year.

The position of the nest-box and the direction of the entry-hole is of paramount importance to some people if a certain pair of birds refuses to go to nest. It is surprising how a pair can be induced to breed just by moving a nest-box a short distance, or even by providing a baffle to the entrance hole.

All birds are individuals and certain things may prove to be a stimulant to one Splendid - or even to a whole group - but may not prove to be to others who require something a little different An amazing amount of knowledge may be acquired just by sitting in your birdroom or alongside your aviary and "just plain lookin'"! Forget the troubles and strifes throughout the world and just enjoy *being* for a while. To some people this may appear to be a complete waste of time, but the amount of pleasure and information made available to us all more than makes up for a little lost time. Various books, magazines, Cage Bird Societies and visits to other bird fanciers are all methods by which we can obtain the answers to the small or large problems that sometimes beset us and we have had occasions in the past to be only too grateful for the availability of them all.

KILLERS

Very occasionally one will breed a Splendid which, if human, would be referred to as a psychopathic murderer or cannibal. These types of specimens are also found among many other kinds of birds and animals but the only one we have had knowledge of was a cock Splendid owned by a friend of ours, who systematically terrorised, killed and endeavoured to rend to pieces any hen unfortunate enough to be put with him. He was a beautiful specimen and the owner, desiring to have youngsters from him, had tried him with hens which behaved towards their fellows in a like manner, hoping they would treat this particular cock in a similar way and perhaps stop his vicious behaviour, but all to no avail. This bird was eventually banished to a mixed aviary containing birds all larger than himself and no further attempt was made to breed with him.

Some of the larger Australian parrakeets treat their partner hens in an abominable fashion and one method used to control these cockbirds would be to clip the feathers of one wing, which would put them off-balance and render them less able to terrorise their hens.

Elder
(Sambucus nigra)

LIGHTING IN THE BIRDROOM

Many different types of lighting may be used to advantage in a birdroom, ranging from a single wall or ceiling bulb for use in a small room, to very elaborate systems incorporating fluorescent tubes connected to time switches, dimmers and electronic light meters.

We use various systems but, basically, what is needed is enough light to enable the Splendids to behave as if in normal daylight. Birds, in general, are secretive creatures which retire to a quiet and dimly-lit retreat in which to lay their eggs and rear a family. In our opinion a room is too bright for really successful breeding if the lighting employed makes the room far brighter than it is normally during daylight hours.

In our 20ft-long birdrooms we employ two 5ft fluorescent tubes for general lighting after dark and an adjustable dimmer switch to provide dusk and dawn lighting. A 5-watt nightlight is used to provide enough light to enable the Splendids to regain their perches should anything cause a disturbance during the hours of darkness. This could be anything from a passing car (where an aviary is sited facing a road or driveway), as the headlamps can give a lightning-like effect as they flash across the windows, to owls hooting or someone walking past the aviaries. In short, anything out of the ordinary can cause night-fright among your Splendids.

In all the years we have been keeping birds we have never yet passed our birdrooms at night and found all the Splendids asleep. It appears as though they "cat-nap" rather than go into a deep sleep. It is possible that this is nature's way of ensuring their survival in the wild, as they are alerted by any strange noise in their immediate vicinity.

Bright lighting is not required for an ailing bird, as any sick bird or animal seeks a dark and secluded spot in which to retire and recover. Obviously any individual or group of birds will become accustomed to very brightly-lit surroundings given time but, in general, you will discover that Splendids in over-lit conditions appear to be a little less steady and at ease than those in softer-lit accommodation.

The brightness of light to aim for is that which is usually found in an aviary with a covered roof on an average Spring or Summer day. It will be noticed that, even under these conditions, your birds will be found to be enjoying the less well-lit corners in which to relax.

In your birdroom aim to provide diffused lighting, if possible, for your Splendids rather than have any number of harsh, glaring electric lightbulbs situated on the wall opposite the breeding cages, thereby shining directly into them. It would be better to have these lights either inside obscure, bulkhead-type containers, or even have a piece of opaque glass or plastic directly in front of them to prevent the harsh glare.

Ceiling lights are best for use in aviaries or shelters, as a bird may attempt to land or perch upon a bare bulb in a wall-mounted socket, with the resulting burns to its feet. It's surprising how hot an electric lightbulb can become, as any of us who have attempted to change a newly-blown bulb can testify! Naked flames of any kind are best not used for lighting - or heating - in a birdroom, due to the possibility of igniting any build-up of feather or other debris that is always present in even the best-kept premises.

We like to put out the main birdroom lights after giving our Splendids a minimum of twelve hours' daylight during their shortest days. The lights are connected through an electric cell, (which switches on and off as the intensity of the daylight increases or decreases), and a time switch to control the number of "daylight" hours available to our birds is also used. We find that a dimmer switch is invaluable when we manually switch off the main birdroom lights, as the room illumination slowly decreases over about twenty minutes, providing the evening "dusk" effect. This period allows the Splendids to "top-up", as it were, with food for themselves and their babies, before retiring for the night.

During the breeding season, (from February until about August for us), the natural dawn awakens the birds, whereupon they begin their foraging process once again.

LITTER FOR FLOOR COVERING in CAGES OR SHELTERS

This is another subject on which the "pros and cons" are many and which is very much a matter of personal preference or availability.

If nothing is used as a floor covering, then one has the arduous task of scraping off any hardened droppings or other debris, and we feel the time taken could be utilised in a much more pleasurable fashion.

Oat husks can be used for the floor of a small cage, or even a larger area if a wide board is fixed around the bottom edge to prevent them being blown away by the bird's energetic wing movements.

Sand, or sawdust is used in some cases, but is liable to be blown around by the Splendids flying from A to B. The fine sand and sawdust may get into the bird's eyes and can cause at the least discomfort, and at the worst serious eye troubles. These disadvantages may be partially overcome by using only a washed, heavy sand or by thoroughly sieving the sawdust so that only a very coarse grade remains. A thickness of at least ½" would have to be used beneath perches to make sure the droppings, especially the ones produced from laying hens, are absorbed and prevented from sticking to the cage floor. Should any of your Splendids decide to bathe and later walk upon a sand-covered floor surface with wet feet, then sand would adhere to them and cause sore, or even cut feet, when the birds stand on the perches later.

Shavings or wood-chips are also available for floor coverings, but it is imperative that neither these, or any sawdust, have ever been in contact with any of the wood preservatives now in general use. We always either make our own, from branches obtained for the fire, or purchase them from a sawmill which uses only locally-grown trees. These we are able to see stacked high in their natural state, many with the bark still on, and we collect our coarse sawdust or wood chips from the machines which render them into planks, etc.

Woodchips also must be sieved to remove all the loose, fine sawdust but they are admirable for the floor of a flight cage, if put down in a deep enough layer. A deeper layer of them must be placed beneath the perches and the heavily-soiled ones can be removed and replaced with clean ones periodically from the main floor. New woodchips can then be used to cover the main floor area once again.

Our favourite material for floor covering in both indoor flights and breeding compartments is newspaper. This we have described fully under **"Birdrooms"**.

Whichever material is decided upon, it is advisable to completely clean the floor area periodically and remove all traces of stale soft food, titbits and soiled seed-husk, etc. Finally, wipe down the entire surfaces and perches with a diluted mixture of disinfectant to prevent the build-up of any disease. We feel precautions like this, which do not take up too much time, go a long way towards preventing any trouble that may take a long time and a lot of hard work and money to clear up.

Do, however, use great care with the handling of any cleaning fluid or disinfectants, and read the instructions carefully. Many people have suffered from various skin complaints by not wearing rubber gloves whilst using some of these products, or by neglecting to use the correct dilutions. Using these articles at double the recommended strength does not necessarily kill double the bugs, but it could do more harm than good to you or your Splendids. Just think of one of your Splendids rubbing its beak or eye along a perch recently wiped over with one of the modern chlorinated bleaches or disinfectants used in the wrong proportions!

One of the reasons we chose newspaper for floor covering in our cages is that on occasions it may be possible to have invasions or build-ups of a noxious little insect called Red Mite. This is a minute, grey, powdery-like insect that our Splendids could either catch from wild birds or they could possibly be brought in on a newly-purchased stock bird.

These insects generally hide away during the day in crevices and emerge at night to feed off the blood of the birds. After enjoying themselves they take on a reddish hue, due to the blood they have consumed, and then leave their host once more to hide away.

We feel that, by using sheets of newspaper for floor-covering, an admirable refuge is provided between the top sheets. By regularly removing the newspapers, burning them and painting any cracks in the cages with one of the proprietary mite destroyers, we keep our birdrooms clear of these pests.

We have yet to see any of these mites on our premises and we like to think that our system of husbandry is responsible for this.

Raspberry
(*Rubus idaeus*)

MASTER COCK OR HEN

In all forms of livestock breeding, one will become aware that some specimens carry certain characteristics which are passed on to the progeny. These are called dominant characteristics and will be evident throughout a particular strain until it is suppressed or altered by a pairing with another specimen also carrying a normally dominant factor. One must take dominance over the other which, in turn, becomes recessive (or hidden, in this instance). The bird which exhibits this prized ability of being repeatedly dominant becomes the Master.

When you are attempting to upgrade your Splendids study your birds and you will discover that one particular cock or hen possesses the above qualities for a factor, or a quality, which is pleasing to your eye. If, for example, a condition known as a "hinged tail" - where the bird's tail hangs vertically and is not held in line with its body - is in evidence in an otherwise nicely turned-out bird, it can be corrected in the young if the bird in question is paired to one which carries its tail in an exaggerated raised fashion. This is known as "evening-out" and a bird carrying any major fault like this should not be used as a master cock or hen. Once your master Splendid has been identified, pair it with as many of your best birds of the opposite sex as you are able and try to spread its good points among as many young as possible. Among your youngsters will be a few which come up to your expectations and these will form your top team in future breeding attempts.

When you breed a specimen which, in your opinion, surpasses its parents in quality and style, this one will take the Master position and the breeding programme can be repeated. We do not like parent-to-offspring or brother-to-sister pairings and would resort to them only on very rare occasions, but breeding with other close relatives is quite acceptable.

Very often it will be found that Splendids excel in one particular feature and strains of birds are bred which, while not themselves possessing that certain visual quality you may consider *par excellence*, will be perfectly capable of producing young which will exhibit the sought-after attributes if a pairing is made of one bird from each strain.

MICE, RATS AND OTHER VERMIN

When designing or building any structure to hold your Splendids, it is wise to take sufficient care to prevent the entry of the various forms of vermin which could possibly cause them harm. By putting ½" wire-mesh on the wooden framework, you would find this sufficient to keep out rats, adult mice, stoats, weasels and grass snakes if you are adjacent to open grasslands or wooded areas. Make sure, however, that the timber is fixed to a concrete or slab foundation to prevent them from burrowing under the wire.

Remember, also, that if you have an earth or gravel floor and a mole decided to come up inside your flight, any of the vermin mentioned could use its tunnel to enter the aviary. If vermin are persistent in your particular area, it might be advisable also to lay ½" wire-mesh over the earth floor.

Our birdrooms are constructed off the ground so that we have access to the area beneath. We keep pots of rat and mice bait under each birdroom at all times and, as soon as we find one empty, it is refilled. Many people put down one or other of the obtainable baits and forget to renew it when the pot is empty. This practice kills off a number of the vermin, but those which ate only a small amount will only become ill. Those which recover from this sickness will become partially immune to the particular material used in the bait and would eventually be totally unaffected by it. These are the so-called "super" mice and rats one hears or reads about in the media and a new drug is needed to subdue them.

Make sure that the doors and windows of your birdroom fit properly and prevent the vermin from entering. This also applies to the inner wire safety-door, which would be in use when your main entry door is open.

Keep all spare seed in metal or strong plastic bins and the floor area clean and free from clutter. This will enable you to detect immediately if any little visitor arrives and decides to take up residence within. Break-back type mousetraps can also be set in hidden corners, but cover them with a leaning tile or similar object to prevent any escaped Splendids in the room becoming trapped.

Cats and hawks can also prove to be a nuisance in some areas but, if the roofs of your aviaries are covered with plastic sheets and the outside walls are double-netted, they will be unable to get into contact with the Splendids. The birds will soon disregard the cats but hawks are another matter. If they prove to be a real menace, two things we have tried appear to reduce, if not eliminate the hazard to our Splendids:

1. During the most troublesome period - the Splendid breeding season - and when the fledglings are most vulnerable to injuring themselves through sheer panic, we hang a sheet of fine horticultural plastic netting loosely over the sides of the aviaries.

2. We have also set up plastic owls in strategic positions, in the old belief that the presence of one predator will deter another.

Although the breeding season of our birds also loosely coincides with the predatory hawk's, we are of the opinion that our actions have prevented most, if not all the hunting over our garden aviaries.

MILLET SPRAYS

These are a valuable source of food for both the young and adult Splendids. They may be fed dry or as a soaked seed and will be avidly consumed either way.

We feed about 1½" to 2" long sections of millet spray to our pairs with young daily, but we do not feed it *ad lib*, as the young birds during the weaning period will feed solely on the millet if available, and completely disregard the other seeds provided. Millet only, possessing as it does less protein than, for example, canary seed, would not prove to be a seed on which the birds would thrive. By limiting it as we do the young Splendids have to try most of the foods offered, thereby obtaining a far more balanced diet.

The sprays, together with any soft food, provide a very good medium with which the birds can be fed any medication if you do not wish to catch them and present the medicine to their beaks. The medicine to be used can be mixed directly with the soft food and we find this method preferable, as the dose can be exactly determined, but millet sprays could be soaked as a last resort and it would give your birds access to some of the prescription.

MIXING STOCK

The mixing of young stock, cocks with hens, is a good idea as it gives them all a chance to mingle, to determine the various pecking orders, and goes a long way towards preventing a brother/sister pair-bond, which we feel is undesirable. The natural playing together, chasing and general *melée* that takes place, all help in the building of strong muscles, control of flight and the overall physical development of the juveniles. They will copy each other and, like all children, will attempt to steal another's playthings or food and, in this way, will taste more of the available titbits provided. This will assist them in obtaining a balanced diet far more than just being in small family groups.

As they develop and become more adult, showing their full colours, then the squabbling will become more serious and the dominant cocks must be separated from the group containing hens before they cause serious injury to each other.

We have discovered that Splendids born around early April or May will commence moulting after they are about six months of age and all will be in adult plumage by the end of the year, but the second round birds will, in most cases, not complete their moult until late Spring the following year.

The first moult is an incomplete moult, with the head having a green central panel over the top and down the neck, merging with the shoulders. The general body area will have acquired adult plumage but the long flight and tail feathers are rarely dropped at this time.

During the second full moult, in late Winter or early Spring, when the Splendids are about eighteen months to two years old, then the whole of the cock's head will attain its fabulous irridescent colours and its scarlet breast will reach its full size and colouring.

Rapid changes of weather and temperature will also cause the birds to go into a partial moult and fill your birdroom with feathers, but these last for a very short while and, if occurring in the middle of the breeding season, will not necessarily cause a pair to desert young or abandon their breeding activities.

During the moulting season all of our game-fishing friends come a-visiting and the various coloured feathers are in great demand for use in the construction of artificial fishing flies. It is quite amazing how one hobby is so closely related to another.

MUTATIONS

A mutation is caused by sudden change in one or more of the chromosomes, sometimes involving an alteration of a single gene; sometimes even affecting a number of chromosomes, or whole sections. This can occur either spontaneously or through radiation and affect the gene's hereditary properties.

Mutations have been occurring since the dawn of time. They have had a great deal to do with natural selection and have assisted in evolutionary change. Very few of these mutations are advantageous and most of the organisms affected by them do not survive for long in the wild.

For example, should an all-yellow Splendid appear among a wild flock, the odds on its survival would be virtually nil, as the first hawk chancing upon the group and intent on a meal would immediately target the yellow bird which would be so conspicuous among its slightly more sombre-coloured fellows.

The component parts of the chromosomes are carrying the building blocks of life, which control the entire make-up of the Splendid and pre-determine everything about it from the length, colour and shape of its bill, through the intensity of body colour, position and soundness of all its internal organs, to the number and shape of each interlocking barb in the construction of its tail feathers.

The Splendids we see before us today are the result of a countless number of mutations or occurrences of a new form, differing from the parents, as a result of changes in the gene-structure in a reproductive cell. Many of these produced would possess new qualities that in some way assisted the species to survive and pass on its new attributes to its offspring.

A number of Australian birds have proved to be exceedingly mutable, including the Budgerigar, Zebra Finch and the Gouldian Finch, which are all now available in a wide range of colours. Although the overall shape of the species remains the same, the size has increased over and above that of their wild cousins. This has been brought about by selective breeding, we believe, rather than by the larger specimens being mutants.

Many of the normal-coloured species carry mutated genes in a recessive form and will only produce their mutant offspring when paired with a mate who also carries this hidden attribute. In the wild the chances of a pair of birds or animals coming together, each with perhaps a newly-mutated reproductive gene which controls exactly the same feature, must be millions to one against.

With birds like the Splendid, being bred under controlled conditions and with a greatly-reduced gene-pool to draw from, the chances of this happening should obviously be more likely. However, if - by inbreeding for many generations - we were able to bring any of these hidden attributes together and produce beneficial mutant young, we would still have to rear them and many new mutations prove difficult, as they would have to be fertile and live long enough to produce a crop of young. These would have to be paired back to their parents to fix the new feature and produce more offspring with which to found a new line or strain. Brother-to-sister breeding could also achieve the same results. (Just imagine all this happening by chance among a flock of wildings!)

During the years of high sunspot activity, more radiation would be directed at the earth and, likewise, the increase of gene alteration within the birds' bodies and it will be interesting to see if a higher than usual number of new coloured Splendids appears after the unfortunate occurence at Chernobyl during April 1986.

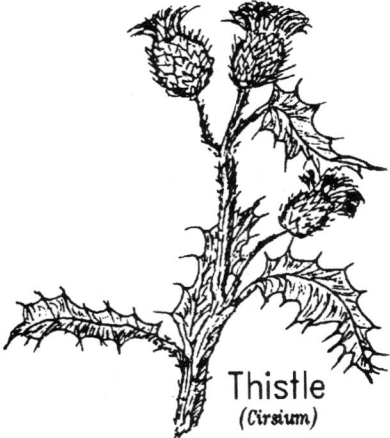

Thistle
(Cirsium)

NEGLECT

One essential piece of information of which anyone who wishes to keep a pair of Splendids should be made aware is that these delightful little treasures, together with any other species of bird or animal, do not take kindly to any form of neglect.

If you are unable to spare the time to give your Splendids the care and attention they so richly deserve, it would be far better for the birds - and for you - if you admired them from afar in some other fancier's collection. Splendids do not, in our experience, require any "mollycoddling", but a few basic requirements must be adhered to.

1. Some of them are susceptible to eye troubles, so perches and the wire-mesh, or other surfaces close to perch-ends, must be kept clean, as the little birds are quite fastidious regarding the cleanliness of their beaks and faces in general. After feeding or bathing, they can be observed wiping their beaks and faces on the surfaces mentioned above to remove any surplus food or water. If these areas are not regularly cleaned, stale food, etc., could be transferred from them - together with any infection - to the bird's face or eyes. This, we are sure, is the origin of many eye troubles among Splendids.

2. Splendids are hardy creatures and, in the wild, are subjected to a wide daily range of temperatures. On occasions these can range from freezing or below overnight to around 70°F or 80°F during the day. They are, however, unable to withstand draughty or continuously damp conditions and this must be taken into account when you are considering their housing.

Our birdrooms, outside the start of the breeding season, are not heated and a few years ago the temperature recorded within one of them was -12°C. All our birds were bursting with health and, when the popholes to the outside flights were opened, they all dashed out to disport in the snow, just like children.

During the Autumn and Winter-time, our birds are all allowed access to outside flights during the day but are shut into their shelters overnight. The only occasions when they are "confined to barracks" are during foggy weather.

3. We like to wash all food utensils at least weekly and the seed mixtures in the dishes are de-husked daily and sieved to remove all dusty debris every couple of days, depending upon the number of birds kept together.

All food used should be fresh and sweet-smelling - no mustiness or dampness - and you should satisfy yourself that any green food offered is free from contamination by either animals or chemical sprays of any kind.

4. If you are a little experimental with titbits, you can "ring the changes" with the various offerings and, besides presenting your Splendids with an interesting diet, this will also go a long way towards preventing them from adopting any vices, such as feather-plucking, to which they may resort through sheer boredom.

A few minutes each day, or longer if you so desire, spent attending to your Splendids (as they will be entirely dependent upon you for everything to sustain them) will be returned a hundredfold in the sheer pleasure they can afford you with their company.

NERVOUSNESS

The majority of Splendids we have bred in a birdroom have been "rock-steady", confiding and trusting. However, a bird will occasionallly be produced which is almost a complete nervous wreck! Perhaps it is the offspring of a pair of birds which have been aviary-bred and may be a little apprehensive at being used for breeding inside a birdroom and in a far closer relationship than it has been accustomed to.

When a nestling like this appears at first in the base of the cage, it will scuttle away to the darkest corner, where it will commence to squeak and continue to do so even after you have left the room. Nestlings will occasionally make a similar noise upon being disturbed within the box, but they generally cease this behaviour upon their entry into the outside world.

Occasionally a bird will continue this action into adulthood and there is nothing more annoying than having this happen each and every time you enter your birdroom to work, or merely to sit and watch them, which is something we feel that many of us enjoy doing.

Nothing we do seems to stop a bird behaving in this fashion, except to place it in an aviary where it does not come into such close contact with people and can retire to its shelter upon anyone's approach.

NEST-BOXES

The standard nest-box in use at the **Buckover Bird Sanctuary** in Gloucestershire is constructed of ½" thick plywood and is 8" x 8" by 8" high, with a removable top and a 5" x 4" door in either the side or back, to enable us to attend to the eggs or nestlings. We prefer not to use the loose top for this purpose, as the hen may feel threatened when the lid is removed from her world and, in her panic, may cause herself or the contents of the nest serious harm when trying to escape through the entry hole (1¾" or 2" diameter).

The nest-box contains a large concave, hollowed from 1" thick softwood, on which is sprinkled a liberal handful of coarse sawdust or crushed woodchips. This material provides the hen with some litter to work, chew, (or throw out) before she begins to lay. We find that these activities, in which the cock will sometimes participate, will assist in the pair-bonding and also bring the hen into a peak of excitement and breeding condition.

Our nest-boxes are hung on to the outside of the breeding compartments, so that the Splendids are able to leave them by moving away from us. When we used to breed all our large collection of Parrakeets in outside aviaries, we had nest-boxes affixed to the aviary walls with the entrance holes facing into the flight, thereby ensuring semi-darkness within. Upon the boxes being opened the birds would scrabble and circle the interior, searching for an escape route away from us, rather than approach the entrance hole that happened to be in the side nearest to us. We soon learnt from our original mistakes.

NOMADISM

In their wild state Splendids are known to travel very little from their selected range, except in seasons of an extra-long drought, when they obviously would go walkabout in search of food, travelling in small groups.

However, it appears strange to us that, whenever a bird escapes - and it is invariably a young, unmoulted bird that attempts this at Buckover - it makes straight for the Welsh hills and we have never regained one yet! Perhaps they are like homing pigeons and, having made a wide, circular flight, head straight back to Australia.

NON-BREEDING HENS

Various methods are advocated in assisting reluctant hens to go to nest. These include fixing bark to the front of nest-boxes; having the nest-boxes in a leaning position on the wall, so the Splendids would enter by walking down a ramp into the box; making sure the entrance-hole faces East; or the use of natural, hollow logs of various sizes.

We find with our Splendids that, providing the matched pair are compatible and in condition, we have difficulty in preventing our hens from laying in the food pots if we do not set up the nest-boxes early enough for their liking!

This behaviour also occurs among the unmatched hens, should they approach breeding condition before we are ready for them.

Should you possess a likely stock hen from which you hope to breed and you are experiencing difficulty in inducing her to go to nest, try to obtain two or three cocks and very carefully introduce her to the flight or cage containing them. Under **no** condition leave the birds in this situation because, providing the cocks are in breeding condition, one particular bird will take the opportunity to "show off" in front of the hen and stake a claim over her. This will be shown in his behaviour towards the other cocks present, which will all be driven away from the hen.

The cock, together with the hen, must be separated immediately from the remainder of the cocks, or a tragedy may occur. Within a few days at the most you will know whether the male's feelings are reciprocated or not.

If the pair do not agree, split them up for a few days before attempting the selection procedure once more, without the first cock being present.

One of the attractions of being a member of a bird club during this time is that you should be aware of perhaps two or three members who also breed Splendids and may be experiencing the same difficulties as yourself. They may be amenable to a suggestion of bringing all the birds together and permitting the Splendids to select their own mates. This would be far more satisfactory than allowing at least one breeding season to be wasted by all of you.

A similar procedure could be carried out with a reluctant male Splendid, but in our experience this is a rather rare occurence!

Cotoneaster franchetii

OVERCROWDING

Overcrowding Splendids in cages or aviaries is something to be on guard against at all times. During the breeding season this is almost bound to happen at one stage or another but, when it does, split the birds up into more manageable units as soon as possible to prevent disease or losses.

As mentioned before, Splendids do not usually form large flocks in the wild and are liable to panic or attack each other if under too much stress occasioned by overcrowding.

Splendids are not in the least like Budgerigars which can perch together, row after row, in almost perfect harmony. In our experience they can and do possess quite a strong territorial instinct, especially the cocks and, in an aviary full of males only, one or two will begin to exhibit this trait by driving away any of their companions which even attempt to occupy not only the same perch, but even the same block of perches.

In our establishment we found that an area consisting of a 10' x 4' inside flight, with access into a 10' x 10' outside flight, could only hold a maximum of twelve to fifteen Splendids, although the available perches could have accommodated many more birds of a different species. The only time it was possible to cage the birds at a higher density was for a short while outside the breeding season and whilst they were moulting. Generally, the birds nearing the completion of the moult (and, therefore, approaching breeding condition) would decide that they required their companions' space rather than their company! This would then entail their removal from the communal flight into a breeding aviary or compartment.

When any birds are in a large group, care must be taken to ensure utensils and surroundings are kept scrupulously clean and a sharp watch kept for any ailing member, which must be removed immediately to prevent any sickness spreading like wildfire.

OBSERVATIONS

Any time spent sitting quietly enjoying your Splendids could prove very beneficial in learning many things about the birds which will assist in better feeding methods and general husbandry, or may perhaps also keep them from danger and help them to live longer. You may, for instance, notice that a section of the aviary has started to rust due to water having dripped continuously onto it and, has deteriorated to such a degree that the bird could escape, or vermin could gain entry.

Various experiments could be made with the addition of different kinds of foodstuffs. You may, for example, provide your Splendids with some Cotoneaster berries, discover that they refuse to eat them, and assume that the birds dislike them. Close observation of your birds may show you, however, that one of their favourite, regular foods has been given in such quantities that the birds have gorged on them to such an extent that there is no room in their crops for anything else. Feeding very small portions of extras and ringing the changes regularly will allow plenty of scope for the introduction of new foods.

Many of us can spend all day looking, and see nothing really new; whilst another person can visit and notice something new instantly.

To watch a Splendid cock display to his hen and offer her some small delicacy is perfectly delightful. He will execute little hops and skips, fan his tail beneath his mate, and almost invite her to dance.

The hen, newly-entered into an aviary or breeding compartment, begins to bow her head and press her beak to many objects within. She appears almost to "sniff", and whether this is in an attempt to discover if another female has made it her territory, or to leave a new scent to mark her own territory, we do not know. Perhaps some other observant fancier of Splendids can let us know the answer.

Very early signs that a bird is ailing may also be spotted and action taken to remedy this. It often happens that we see in print a report of some new discovery regarding bird behaviour and we say to ourselves, "Well! That isn't new - I have known about that for ages!" We have just accepted the fact that a certain action takes place, yet it hadn't been made common knowledge.

A small notebook is invaluable to keep a permanent record of any unusual occurences and it can be referred to at any time.

When you visit other fanciers to purchase new stock, observe the husbandry practiced and size and type of nest-boxes. Then, by using similar equipment during later breeding activities, using your newly-acquired stock, you should have a much better chance of a successful season.

OPTIMISM

Anyone who embarks on the breeding of any form of livestock, including Splendids, must be an optimist. As any breeders can testify, during their years of working with livestock they will have successful years and disappointments. We all do.

We can all obtain the best stock available, provide ideal quarters and supply a perfectly well-balanced diet. Even so, with the best will in the world, it will be found that some years we can do nothing wrong and our stock will breed well and produce a bumper crop of lovely youngsters, whereas another year, treating them in exactly the same way will produce disastrous results and analysing everything we did will supply us with no valid reason for this occurring. Luckily, this happens very rarely, but we still feel that the bottom has dropped out of our world.

This kind of hazard is forever present but some people still hopefully start with large breeding establishments. Although they have had no previous experience of breeding livestock, they expect to make their fortunes, or at least become instantly on a par with some of the country's larger and most successful breeders. When this type of person experiences one or two years of mediocre results in return for a lot of hard work and expense, they often decide to cut their losses and quit the business. We have observed and experienced in the past that it pays dividends to start in a small way and, over a number of years, gain experience in the breeding of Splendids and learn to overcome the disappointments we will all share at some time or another. Do not over-extend yourself, especially when commencing in our delightfully satisfying hobby and, if you do wish to expand, do so slowly .

"Lady Luck" plays a large part in our hobby, together with the optimism that we have sensed and seen among the many friends we have in the world of breeding Splendids. Normally we all experience reasonable results during the breeding seasons, as Splendids are one of the freer-breeding members of the *NEOPHEMA* family and we meet very few real problems but, on the occasions when things do go wrong, breeders generally say "Ah, well! Next year, if I put that cock with this hen into a different aviary, it might prove to be the answer to the problem."

Join our clan, and welcome! Within a few years or so you, too, will repeat the words written above.

OBJECTIVE

Everyone who enters our hobby must have some objective, whether it be to enjoy the sights and sounds emanating from a small, mixed aviary; or with the intention of creating their own strain of Splendids with which to enter into - and win in - the world of exhibition. Challenges will be met and overcome and many good friends are available in whichever sections of bird-keeping you decide to embark upon. Set your sights as high as you please and, if your hobby of breeding Splendids provides you with half as much pleasure and half as many friends as we have been lucky enough to achieve, you will not be doing too badly.

PAINTING CAGES

The painting of stock cages, show cages and breeding units in birdrooms is, in our view, of paramount importance. Apart from the pleasing appearance it provides, it ensures that all small crevices that could harbour mites, or other "little visitors", are filled and sealed with paint, thus preventing infestation of your Splendids.

We use a non-gloss emulsion paint for the interior of all our units, as a gloss paint (although likely to last longer) can act like a mirror and can cause distress or irritation to the inmates if they can see what they believe to be a rival in such close proximity. We have also noticed birds in a cage with a high gloss finish twirling their heads in a complete circle, following the numerous reflections, until they fall off the perch. These action cease when they are removed from the glossy cage and placed into one with a dull finish. If two or more coats or paint are applied, we find that the walls can be washed down each year, and we renew the paint around every third year.

The lining of birdrooms with a laminated material, to dispense with having to paint at all, is now practiced and, as long as it can be obtained in a non-gloss finish, it does provide an admirable finished surface - providing that all cracks and joints can be sealed against mites.

We use a white emulsion paint because it reflects the light so well and helps to lighten up the whole birdroom, but pastel shades may be preferable for some people and would certainly be less harsh and clinical.

PARASITES

Internal and external parasites may attack your Splendids on occasions. When aviary breeding is practiced it is more difficult to prevent re-infestation after treatment, as wild birds often come and feed from feeding platforms which can be reached from both inside and outside the enclosures. Under these circumstances, it would appear that the only thing to do may be to regularly dust the interior of the nest-boxes with one or other or the anti-mite preparations which can be obtained from pet shops and seed suppliers. We prefer a *Pyrethrum*-based insecticide for our Splendids, but this is purely a matter of personal preference as there are plenty of others which you can use with perfect safety.

Aviary hygiene should be practiced by removing all stale vegetable matter, if fed to your birds, as slugs and snails could be attracted to this and these molluscs act as hosts for some of the parasitic internal worms which are liable to infect your Splendids.

On occasions mites of the *Arachnid* family may also be passed on to your Splendids from the wildings and these may be seen, if present, sliding between the feathers of a wing, or on the rump. They should be removed by catching the birds and thoroughly dusting them with a safe insecticide, but this is not advisable while young nestlings are within the nest-box and being fed. Whilst breeding in birdrooms, there is less likelihood of parasite infestations if the breeding compartments and the birds are treated at the beginning of the nesting season.

"PASSENGERS"

These may be Splendids of either sex which steadfastly refuse to breed, season after season, regardless of what you do. We consider that any bird which has made no attempt to breed for the first two seasons of its life is not suitable for inclusion within a stud. No bird which suffers from this condition should be sold to another fancier unless he or she is made aware of this fact, although moving to a new owner and a fresh environment can quite often trigger off the breeding cycle.

PERCHES

In cages, or aviaries, try to supply a variety of perches, both thick and thin. Natural ones such as Hazel or Willow wands are to be preferred to prepared, hardwood dowelling, as the naturable variable ones allow the feet to flex to a different position each time the Splendids land. This exercises the toes and the twigs are also springy, which enables the birds to alight in a gentle fashion. Hardwood perches jar the bird's legs and frame when it comes to a sudden halt upon landing.

Perches set at varying angles, instead of all being horizontal, are also much used by the Splendids. The birds can be observed running up and down and providing themselves with plenty of exercise, which does much to prevent the boredom so often seen in some collections.

In our aviaries we also provide thicker, semi-rotten branches in which our Splendids spend hours excavating small or large holes and investigating the cracks in the bark. We use mostly deciduous fruit tree or willow branches and, of course, any *Eucalyptus* timber that comes our way, but we never use Yew or any other known, or suspected, poisonous wood. If you are in any doubt whatsoever, do not use it. Almost any nursery or garden centre should be able to advise you which local timber would be safe for you to use.

Square softwood perches are suitable for use, providing the sharp corners are slightly rounded and the timber used has **not** been treated with any preservative or insecticide.

Hardwood dowelling is generally available and used for perches. either round or oval being obtainable, but it soon acquires a natural, iron-hard sheen and the birds frequently find it difficult to hold their grip on it and successfully mate. Try, if possible, to slightly roughen the surface of the perches with a very coarse grade sand or emery-paper to assist the Splendids to secure a hold on them and maybe fill more eggs for you!

PETS

The temperament of many of the Splendids of our acquaintance would make the little bird an ideal pet and companion.

This would not apply to all Splendids, and the young birds selected for pets would have (in general) to come from steady parents which are used to the close proximity of people and which don't panic when they are placed into a smaller cage than that to which they have been accustomed.

As mentioned earlier, we discovered when we first decided to breed our Splendids under cover, in 5' long compartments instead of their usual 6' long outside flights, that a percentage of our birds proved completely incapable of settling down to the situation of being unable to escape from the proximity of humans. They would immediately fly to the furthest point in the cage away from us, upon our entry into the birdroom, and would commence to squeak in a most annoying fashion. This persisted as long as we were in their vicinity.

Any youngster displaying this characteristic or, in our view, bred from parents with a similar disposition, would be unsuitable for a house pet.

Some aviary-bred Splendids and, we have found, most of those bred inside a birdroom in breeding compartments of steady and confiding parents, would prove to be suitable for a pet and would give much pleasure and companion-ship to their owners in return for the care and affection spent on them.

One Splendid which we kept indoors proved to be a most endearing little creature and many happy years were spent enjoying its presence. It had a pleasant little song - if you could call it that - and, with its single, melodious note of alarm, it would give us ample warning if any neighbour's cat appeared on the lawns near the outside aviaries. We spent many hours with it free in our sitting room and it could always be returned to its cage on the production of a short length of millet spray, whereupon it would fly to the hand and clamber around. Both seed spray and bird could then be placed together within the cage. It would also return of its own free will after an interval of flying around the room investigating everything in sight that appeared to be edible.

A young Splendid chosen for a house pet should be one that has been handled in the nest-box. This should continue whilst it remains in the breeding cage with its siblings and parents until weaned. This early steadying will stand it in good stead later when it is on its own in the house. Young cocks or hens will both make agreeable pets if alone but, in pairs, may occasionally become fractious - as will all types of pet - when the urge to breed is upon them.

The most suitable cage in a house would be a single or double Budgie breeding cage. This is a plywood box, either 63cms x 47cms by 29cms deep, or 127cms x 47cms by 29cms deep - the longer of the two having a removable slide situated in the centre to divide it into two compartments. The breeding cage is enclosed on all sides except for the front, which is made of wire and possesses a large door in the centre. In the base of each compartment is a removable tray for ease of cleaning.

On purchasing your treasure, place it in its cage, together with food and water, and leave it to its own devices for a day or two. This will enable it to settle down in its new home and regain its feeling of security.

When feeding and watering daily, leave your hand within the cage for lengthening periods of time and introduce a short length of millet spray to the bird. It should soon begin to feed off the spray whilst it is still being held by you.

Remember that very few birds of any kind relish being held in a closed hand, so it would be preferable if the Splendid was not handled, but tempted to stand on your finger and eat the millet.

If the nestling is prevented from leaving its cage until it accepts your finger as a perch, and is carefully taken from one wooden perch to another within the cage without fear, it should be possible to open the cage door, after making sure that all doors, windows, etc., are closed, and allow it to make its own way out into the room.

This is best done in the evening, when curtains will cover the windows and thus prevent any injuries caused by the bird flying at full speed into the glass. Only when the Splendid is really familiar with your living room would it be advisable to slowly reveal the window-glass.

Should your pet prove unwilling to perch on your finger and be returned to its cage, a towel would prove useful to drop over the bird to secure it. If this fails, wait for it to settle, darken the room, then slowly approach to make your capture.

POST MORTEMS

Should you suffer the unexplained loss of any Splendids, unless the cause of death was obviously through an injury, it is wise to contemplate sending the bird off to a veterinary laboratory for analysis, especially if it was a member of a larger group or unit. In this way any possible infectious condition could be arrested by the immunisation of its erstwhile companions.

This action is much preferable to losing a number of birds before taking any action and then discovering that the trouble is harder to eradicate than would have been necessary had swift action been taken initially.

PRECAUTIONS DURING EPIDEMICS

Luckily, only on very rare occasions does an epidemic - such as Ornithosis or Fowl Pest (Newcastle Disease) - strike birds belonging to a member of our hobby.

A member of the veterinary profession must be informed and may order the destruction of all birds on the premises. All cages, utensils and aviaries must be disinfected, preferably by a vet, and no birds will be allowed back on the premises for a certain length of time which will be determined by the veterinary official. The period is generally a minimum of six months, or longer.

It would be completely irresponsible for anyone whose premises are infected in this manner to go visiting other fanciers until cleared by the vet attending the outbreak, and most unwise for another fancier to visit aviaries or birdrooms so affected. If one has to attend (to assist, or for any other reason) the veterinary officer or local Ministry of Agriculture official could recommend a disinfectant to place in a tray, or soak an area of straw through which everyone visiting must paddle in wellingtons, both to go in and to come out.

PROBLEMS

The large majority of Splendid or other bird fanciers have problems at some time or another.

Maybe they have managed to obtain a pair of the birds of their dreams, and find that they have nowhere to house them. This is where friends can come to your assistance by, perhaps, housing one of your other pairs of stock birds for you on a temporary basis, so that you can commence breeding with your "stormers".

Perhaps some other situation arises and a bit of advice may be needed. We have found, during our many years of breeding Splendids, that no-one has all the answers and everyone needs a little help at some time or another.

Do not be afraid to ask advice from any other member of your bird Club or Society and you will be pleasantly surprised at the assistance you will receive. If you are unable to obtain the answer to your problem, you will find magazines, such as *"Cage & Aviary Birds"*, have a section on reader's questions, with a panel of experts to supply the answers to most queries.

Another fountain of knowledge that may be tapped is the large number of specialist breeders who dispose of their stock through advertisements. Visit some of these and, if our experience is anything to go by, you will be welcomed and all the information you require will be freely given. All you need to do is ask, and a problem that appeared to be insurmountable could soon recede to the size of a molehill.

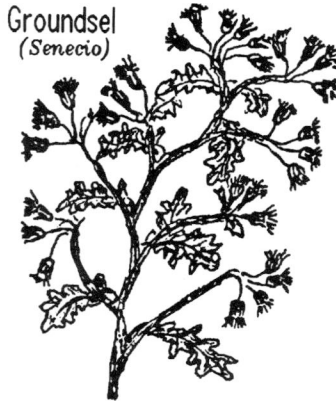

Groundsel
(Senecio)

QUARANTINE

All groups of animals, birds and people carry a body burden of differing "gut flora", obtained from various sources. The large majority of these are benign and either assist in the digestion of food or live off body wastes, etc., causing no harm. The others can cause numerous illnesses to which the body eventually becomes immune, or sometimes dies.

This was proved a few hundred years ago, during the great voyages of discovery, when Europeans carrying diseases such as measles encountered and mixed with natives who had never previously been exposed to this relatively harmless illness. The natives died in their thousands before the few survivors eventually built up an immunity.

A Splendid can add to its own particular gut flora in many ways. First of all, from parents during feeding and whilst in the nest litter. It then leaves the nest and enters a new world, which its explores with its beak - nibbling everything in sight. It will eat dried droppings, from which it obtains the vitamin B12 which it needs and, if in an open aviary, it will be also be exposed to the influences of the wild bird populations.

On leaving its parents it will probably be mixed with other young with a similar body burden and will either build up a wider immunity, or succumb.

When the young Splendid travels from its birthplace to another aviary, it undergoes quite a bit of stress during the travelling and later, when it is placed in unfamiliar surroundings. Stress lowers the bird's ability to fight any infection, so it should be first placed in a cage or aviary on its own, or with one or two companions only. If any cross-infections are likely to occur, they will possibly show up within a few weeks and, if the birds have been kept isolated from your main stock, any possible outbreak will be contained. The practice of regular treatment of all stock with medicants of any kind as a preventative measure does, we feel, more harm than good, as the birds have to build up a new body burden of beneficial gut flora after each session and, until this is once again complete, they are unprotected from many diseases.

QUERIES

Question the standard procedures used as the norm in any breeding or husbandry pattern. Most of the systems found will have been arrived at over many years of trial and error and are probably the correct method to suit the fancier's own requirements. Many actions are taken because the available time spent on a hobby is limited, or perhaps finance plays a large part. Each and every one of us works to a system which is right for us, but newcomers seeing our procedures for the first time would perhaps devise an alternative way of looking after their Splendids.

For example, we use plastic plant saucers for our seed and water containers. They are "cheap and cheerful" and, when any become stained with salts from our water supply, for instance, which are almost impossible to remove, we then relegate them to the greenhouse and replace them with new ones. Other fanciers use feed and water pots made of china or metal, and will have their own reasons for the preference. Some fanciers feed each individual type of seed in a separate container, whilst others feed only mixtures. The variations are endless and each method has a reason for being selected and utilised.

Many nest-box sizes depend upon the personal preference of the individual fancier and they are constructed from a large range of materials, from cardboard to plastic, and each types has its advocates. Methods of breeding Splendids vary, with some fanciers swearing by aviary breeding, whilst others, like us, prefer to breed inside birdrooms and give all our stock access to aviaries outside the breeding season.

Do not blindly follow another's procedures but, by asking questions of many fanciers as to why a certain system has been adopted, you will be in a position to evolve a satisfactory method of your own.

RECORDS

If anyone wishes to take up the breeding of Splendids and continue in a serious manner, they will have to keep records of their endeavours.

These can be of a simple form, consisting of one card for each pair and containing the following information:

1. Cage number.

2. Identifying ring number, or colour of both cock and hen.

3. Year born.

4. Date paired and ring colours used for each particular pair.

5. Date first egg laid and number of eggs.

6. Date due to hatch. (Add 20 days from laying of first egg.)

7. Ring numbers and colours of young.

Repeat this information for each round produced.

Having this information for each pairing will assist you in identifying each bird paired up and so prevent too close inbreeding. You can see at a glance whether a particular pairing or line is fertile and to what degree. This last information is invaluable, as it will make sure you are not repeatedly pairing birds together from a line which consistently produces the odd one or two chicks per season. It is most important to found a strain on the most fertile birds available and, if possible, make this one of your main aims. You will also discover that some lines produce more young of one sex than another, so a blend of these lines is very desirable.

These cards can be kept in a file, or results can be entered in a stud record-book if you so desire, and they will therefore be available for a reference in later years.

When you begin to breed any of the different-coloured Splendids, some method of recording is a must, as you will invariably be producing youngsters which are "split", (or carrying a hidden factor), for the colours you are endeavouring to produce. Without records to refer to, you would soon be in a muddle and unable to assist any prospective purchaser of your stock.

RINGS

There are two types of rings which may be used to identify Splendid Grass Parrakeets. One type is a sealed metal band, made of aluminium, which may be obtained in a colour selected by the makers to correspond with each particular year. These may also be inlaid with the year, consecutive numbers, and your initials. These are known as "closed rings" and the size to fit Splendids and other Grass Parrakeets at the time of writing is **Size L**. They may only be fitted to baby Splendids of between five and ten days old, and it is far better to have a ring slip off a youngster and have to replace it, than leave it too late and find yourself unable to fit the ring over the ball of the bird's foot.

The method we use for closed ringing of our Splendids is as follows; One of us catches the bird and gently but firmly holds it, whilst the other obtains the closed ring and a wooden toothpick or sharpened matchstick. A ring is slipped over the three long toes, over the ball of the foot and up to the hock, trapping the fourth toe along the leg. We insert the toothpick or match between the leg and toe and gently ease the toe out from under the ring. Occasionally a slight lubrication is required during this operation.

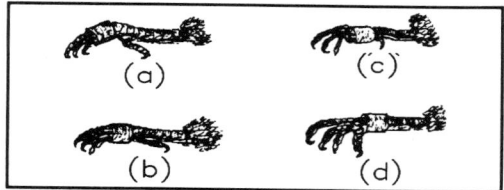

(a) (b) (c) (d)

These rings, when fitted, and when the bird is fully developed, are impossible to remove without cutting them off with metal cutters. They can provide a permanent record of the year of the Splendid's birth, together with any other information you had engraved on the ring. When Splendids fitted with the correct, closed rings are loose in an aviary or flight with others of their kind, there is no danger of the rings slipping off and the bird becoming anonymous. There is a danger, however, of the ring on a very young Splendid becoming encrusted with droppings or other debris deposited on the nest-box base, and this could find its way to the inside of the ring next to the bird's leg, causing constriction or chafing, with unwelcome results. Care must be taken to check leg rings, at the same time as you examine beaks, ceres and toenails for this cement-like substance, and any deposits found should be removed. A toothpick or sharpened matchstick will prove to be a useful tool to carefully carry out this operation.

We prefer, however, to use plastic split-rings for our Splendids. These can be placed on each leg when the young are removed from their parents and released, with their fellows, into flights. The rings, **Size XB** for Splendids and other Grass Parrakeets, are available from various manufacturers who advertise in bird-keeping magazines. They are made in twelve plain colours and 76 striped colours. By using a special tool they can be placed on any bird's leg, regardless of age.

These rings are fitted in the following manner; With the Splendid held firmly by one of us, the other opens the split-ring by sliding it along the shoe-horn shaped fitting tool, which is then placed along the bird's lower leg. With the leg in the groove of the tool, we gently slide the ring from the tool and onto the leg, where the flexibility of the ring will cause it to close around the limb.

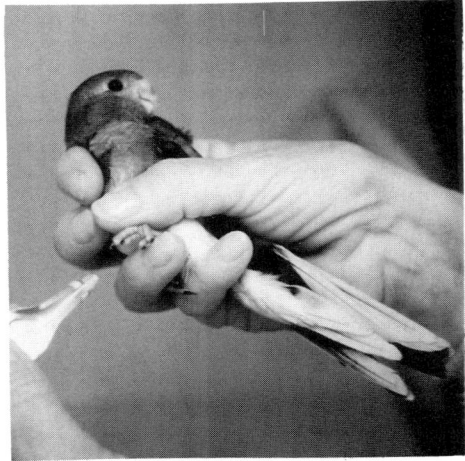

We have discovered that, if the weather and plastic ring are very cold, the ring is inclined to fracture when pressure is applied to open it with the tool provided. We always first warm the rings to prevent this occurring under these circumstances.

We fit two rings, one to each leg. The first is used as a numbered and coloured ring to identify the year and family number and the other is a striped, two-coloured ring to identify the Splendid's family without having to catch the bird first. Should one of these become dislodged, which does happen occasionally, another can be fitted and the records adjusted accordingly. With these split-rings being fitted after the young Splendids have vacated the nest, there is little or no danger of the ring becoming encrusted with droppings, etc., with any of the attendant perils.

SEED

Seed for Splendids must be of the best quality obtainable and must be dust-free. This will pay dividends in the long run, as it should keep your birds free from the respiratory diseases so often associated with stale and dusty seed.

New season seed, if stored under adverse conditions such as a damp atmosphere, or if it has been harvested before it is really ripe, will sweat and soon become mouldy, giving off that strange, almost yeasty smell.

Good seed, if taken in a cupped, double handful, should have a faint, sweet, nutty smell to it, combined with its own individual scent, and there should be no unpleasant odours whatsoever. Some sunflower seeds can have a most unpleasant odour if kept in a dry, closed container for a considerable time, so you should allow air to this seed if possible.

New or old, dead seed that has a very low germination rate is useless as feed for your stock and this seed immediately becomes apparent if a handful is put to soak in a bowl. You will find that, even after agitation, the dead seed will float to the surface of the water and will appear to be almost like husk as it lies there. If you attempt to germinate this light seed, you will find it is impossible to do so.

To test the percentage of germination you can take a random sample of 100 seeds, soak them and leave them in a warm place. Spray them daily for a week or so and, when the shoots have grown approximately ½", count the number of germinated seeds. Seventy-five germinated seeds would equal 75% germination for that particular batch. Personally, we would like to see around 90% germination at least but, with some of the sunflower seed available, we have experienced much lower percentages. Birds will eat infertile seed, if there is nothing else available, but there will be very little or no sustenance in it, thus preventing your stock from thriving.

SECURITY

This comes under two headings. The first will be keeping your Splendids from escaping and includes the fitting of safety doors to your aviaries, flights or birdrooms. Check periodically for the lifting or breaking away of the wire-mesh from the timber frame, owing to the staples rusting or breaking. Timber can shrink, leaving small, inviting slits just right for a hen's inquisitive beak to expose and enlarge.

A useful method of keeping any entrance door closed can be made so simply from a length of wire fixed to the top bar of the door's framework, passing through an easily-obtained pulley inside the safety porch or aviary, with the free end attached to a metal weight or even a brick. This would be raised by the door being opened and the weight, in returning to its original position, would draw the door closed.

The second heading on security deals with the "light-fingered gentry" we unfortunately appear to have in our communities at the present time. *Locks are only meant to keep out honest people*" is a phrase we heard many years ago, and it is still very true. Banks can be secured by many locks and guards, but they are still robbed.

Many types of security systems are available for use in birdrooms and aviaries, as mentioned before, and if possible a good house-dog is a useful back-up. Unless you are inclined to invest in a "Fort Knox" type security system and never leave your premises unguarded, the risk will always be there.

Insurance may be a good idea in many circumstances. However, it does pay to be on the alert for the odd visitor being a little more inquisitive than usual, regarding the methods and types of security devices. If you are really worried, a little time devoted to taking vehicle licence-plate numbers of strangers in your vicinity may help to put your mind at rest. Joining a "Neighbourhood Watch" group is also a very good idea.

SEGREGATION

At the end of the breeding season this works very well for us, as we do our breeding in birdrooms. We split up all our pairs and the hens and cocks spend the Autumn and Winter in separate communal flights for each sex. They are shut in at night, but have unlimited exercise outside during the days and it also seems to help them lose some of the fat they are inclined to acquire whilst rearing their young and living off the best food available - the "fat of the land", so to speak.

In our experience, if the pairs are left together they are inclined to just "sit and think", either together or one at each end of the flight, but in a communal flight much more movement is apparent, with the jockeying for perches or positions within their society.

SELECTION FOR BREEDING & SHOWING

During the period of segregation the majority of the Splendids go through a moult and, with this completed, the birds can be caught up if necessary and compared with each other in a cage at close quarters. Any showing signs of being potential prize-winners can be placed together in a separate flight, left to develop further any exceptional quality, and be trained to display in a showcage. In this way there is less likelihood of disposing of a member of your top breeding team than if the Splendids were all together in mixed groups and in one large flight. If you are intending to compete on the show-bench with your Splendids, this would also be the time to select the birds that appeal to you most. Any Splendids that you consider are of possible show quality should be removed from the main flights and examined carefully for physical defects. Any discovered with missing or broken claws, whilst not being of any use for showing purposes, could still be used for breeding, as there should be no danger of these defects being passed onto their young.

No injuries which occur in the lifetime of a bird can be transmitted genetically to its offspring. Any broken tail or flight feathers should be gently removed at least six or seven weeks before the show in which it will be entered. This should enable it to be completely renewed to its final length.

SEX-LINKED CHARACTERISTICS

A bird's cells present in its make-up contain chromosomes in pairs and each chromosome carries a number of genes which determine the colour and all the other characteristics of the bird, including the sex. The sex-determining pair of chromosomes, XX in the cock and XY in the hen, carry the genes only on the X chromosomes.

During mating, the X chromosome from the hen can unite with either X chromosome in the cock to produce young cocks, or her Y chromosome could unite with either X and produce young hens.

As the Y chromosomes carry no genes, the colour and certain other sex-linked characteristics are carried only on the X chromosomes. The Lutino and Albino colouring and red-eyed phenomenon is an example of sex-linkage. A cock may carry the sex-linkage gene on either both, one, or none of his X chromosomes. If he carries none he is a pure normal.

If he carries it on one X chromosome, he will be a normal-looking bird but carries the hidden factor and will be referred to as a split (sex-linked) Lutino, or whatever. If he carries it on both, he will be a visual Lutino, etc.

If a hen carries no sex-linked gene on her single X chromosome, she will be a pure normal. If she carries the gene on her single X chromosome, she will be a visual Lutino, or whatever other characteristic the gene carried. A normal hen cannot be a carrier of a sex-linked gene, for example, split for Lutino, etc., as the Y carries no genes for this phenomenon.

For example:-

Normal Cock $X + X$ Norman Hen $X + Y$

Lutino Cock $X_1 + X_2$ Lutino Hen X_1 or $X_2 + Y$

Split Lutino Cock $X_1 + X$, or $X_2 + X$

Pairings

Lutino Cock x Normal Hen =   Split Lutino Cocks X_1 or $X_2 + X$
and
Lutino Hens X_1 or $X_2 + Y$

Normal Cock x Lutino Hen =   Split Lutino Cocks $X_1 + X$ or $X_2 + X$
and
Normal Hens $X + Y$

Split Lutino Cock x Normal Hen = Split Lutino and Normal Cocks
and
Lutino and Normal Hens

Split Lutino Cock x Lutino Hen = Lutino and Split Lutino Cocks
and
Lutino and Normal Hens

Lutino Cock x Lutino Hen =   All Lutino young

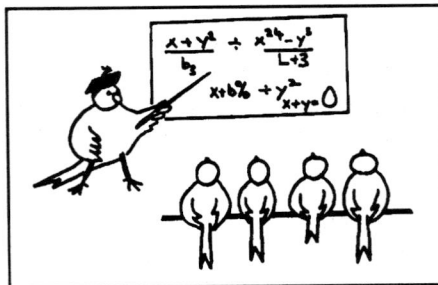

SHOWING SPLENDIDS

There is no set show standard for Splendids at the moment and they are generally shown in with other Australian Grass Parrakeets at many open shows. These exhibits are normally assessed along the following lines and judges, being individuals, will put a greater emphasis on different aspects of the individual birds and, indeed, in some cases on the cages. Some people use a Budgerigar show-cage and others a Foreign Bird show-cage. It would pay you to visit a few shows to see for yourself the competition and type of cage used. It is a complete waste of the judge's time and your effort if your Splendid is messy, or the cage is dirty and unpainted. If your birds are worth showing, they are worth a little extra effort. Check over all your show-cages. Any damaged ones may be used for training purposes and the rest will require washing thoroughly and then repainting in the required colours, normally black and white.

At the show any sick or injured bird would be removed from the show hall immediately and, if any exhibit was nervous or untrained to a show-cage and spent most of its time hidden beneath the water pot, it may prove to be impossible to judge. Time is always spent attempting to induce the odd exhibit to perch correctly and show off its lines and physical attributes, but if it is unwilling or unable to do so for the judge, then it may be that a prospective winner could end up out of the cards. Visitors and owners of birds who visit the show after judging make all sorts of remarks regarding the judge's eyesight, when they see the birds back on the viewing stands and the birds, no longer tense and nervous, are showing themselves off in their natural conditions. No longer is that "stormer" hiding beneath the water pot, but it is up on its perch and standing head and shoulders above the bird which was awarded the red ticket and maybe had its cage covered with rosettes.

The judges, we are afraid, can only go by the state of the exhibits before them and, if one or other of the birds will not perch and display itself, then it must be placed behind those which do, in the order of merit. Having judged at a few shows, we are only too painfully aware that this is the case.

All Splendids being judged would be checked that they are in the correct class, according to the show schedule, and for any obvious damage such as missing or deformed toe-nails, etc. Any discovered to be imperfect in these respects would be put to one side. The condition of the exhibits is then scrutinised and all of those not possessing perfect feather-texture and condition - for example; spikes, or broken or missing flight or tail feathers - would be placed on the right-hand side of the judging table and those with type and in the best condition would be moved to the left.

An exhibition Splendid must possess type and good deportment if it is going to make its mark on the show-bench. This will stand out immediately to anyone who enters a show hall or birdroom. The bird possessing it may be just "sitting there", but one with good type will ooze self-confidence and well-being.

Depth of bib we personally would put next, but whatever the size of the bib we prefer it to be a straight cut-off where it joins the buttercup-yellow underbelly, and not to terminate in a ragged fashion.

If it is a normal exhibit and not a Pied, then there would have to be no mis-marking of the feathers on either body, wings or tail. Overall brightness of colour would then be assessed as, in our view, a Splendid lacking the vibrant colours found only in birds of perfect health and vitality, lacks much of its appeal.

Size in a Splendid is, in our opinion, of reasonable importance but, just because an exhibit was larger than all other competitors, it would not automatically be assured of coming first in its class if others were generally better specimens, but slightly smaller. However, remember the old adage, "*A good big 'un will always beat a good little 'un!*" It is still in vogue.

Oregon Grape
(*Mahonia aquifolium*)

SOFT-SHELLED EGGS

These are occasionally experienced among hens of any age and it would appear to be a lack of calcium in the diet or else the inability of the hen to assimilate the available minerals. If Splendids are fed a good mixed grit *ad lib* and sometimes well-baked and crushed eggshells, there should be no problem with soft-shelled eggs. Great care, however, must be taken to ensure that any domestic hen's eggshells used are washed clean and baked in an oven hot enough to destroy any bacteria that may be present, before crushing and feeding them to your Splendids.

Should none of these treatments work and your hens still produce soft-shelled eggs, it might pay to consult a veterinary surgeon to ascertain whether any of the liquid calcium solutions that are available for animal use may possibly help if administered to your stock.

SPARE HENS

Accidents do happen during the breeding season and losses can sometimes occur. If you have room it is certainly advisable to keep back one or two spare hens at the commencement of the breeding season for use during the above circumstances, or even to replace the hen of a non-compatible pair. This can often prevent a wasted season and, if the spares are not required for your own use, they may be sold to help someone else out later on in the year.

On some occasions a hen might die at the commencement of the breeding season and the owner may not be able to purchase a replacement for financial reasons. Perhaps under these circumstances a few enquiries may locate someone with a spare hen or two who would be prepared to loan one on breeding terms. This would mean that the person breeding from the pair of Splendids, but only owning one of them, would share any young produced with the other owner, say on a 60-40% basis, the 60% share to go to the individual concerned with the actual breeding endeavours.

TRAINING FOR SHOWING

Splendids which are intended to be shown will need to be trained to a show-cage from a very early age. An old show-cage (without its wire front and drinker) in a flight will soon be used by the youngsters for perching in and, providing the floor is regularly cleaned, a few titbits such as sections of millet spray can be placed inside, to induce them all to enter and lose their fear of it.

When your young Splendids are nearing completion of their moult, the most promising ones can be brought into a birdroom and placed into roomy stock cages. A show-cage, complete with its wire front and interior pots, should now be hung on the end of these stock cages and more titbits placed inside. It will soon be found that the birds will enter the show-cages for increasing lengths of time and will investigate them thoroughly.

After a while the show-cages, with a Splendid in residence, can be taken down and, with the door shut, be placed in another part of the birdroom and left for a short while. The majority of your Splendids will remain on the perch when you approach and pick up a show-cage, but a few will jump to the floor and attempt to hide in corners.

If a thin, tapered hazel-nut wand of about 12" to 15" long, or a judging stick, is placed under the belly of the bird and gently lifted, it will be found that the bird will step onto it and can then easily be lifted up to the perch. With enough training of this kind it will be seen that the birds in the cage bottom will spring up to the perches on your approach, or as soon as they see the judging stick. Training of this kind can go a long way towards ensuring your birds will not be discarded by a judge for refusing to perch on request.

Birds travelling to shows and during the judging are subjected to a lot of movement whilst in their cages, so the next step after getting the Splendids used to their cages is to carry the cages around the birdroom, garden and house, and even out in the car to simulate travelling to the show. When you visit shows you will notice how close people will be to your birds so, if possible, you must also acclimatise them to this kind of activity.

Any Splendids which show signs of being distressed or which are of a very nervous disposition during show-training are, in our opinion, best left out of the show-team and returned to the aviaries. We have experienced birds so nervous that as soon as anyone approaches them they begin to growl continuously, and this can be most disturbing for both them and the onlookers.

Some people use carrying cases for their show-cages, so their Splendids have to become accustomed to being carried around in this fashion. All this training, which takes place periodically during the showing season, can enable your birds to swiftly overcome any upset through travelling to the shows and being handled by strangers and they will display themselves boldly to the judges at the appointed time. Doing all we can in this way for our Splendids; training, benching them in a well turned-out show-cage and feeding them on a well-balanced diet, will assist our individual treasure to outshine all others and come home with its cage festooned with rosettes. Showing your Splendid can be a marvellous way in which to meet many new friends with a similar interest to yourself and through whom you will be able to pick up much valuable information regarding our hobby in general.

TRANSPORTING STOCK

When sending or taking Splendids to shows, provision has to be made for feeding the birds. Most show rules insist that birds of individual species are only allowed to have certain foods placed in the cages. In general, for showing Splendids the base of the cage should be covered in a layer of parrakeet mixture only, with no titbits added. If in any doubt, check with the Show Secretary when you apply for your entry forms. Water pots will remain empty and will be filled by Show Stewards after judging is completed.

When sending Splendids by road or rail to our customers we always use a plywood travelling box with a wire grill at one end. Half the top can be unscrewed for inserting or removing the birds. We place plenty of our usual seed mix within to more than allow for any delay during their journey and we also include a length of wet millet spray to provide moisture during the journey. The millet sprays are always previously soaked for 24 hours and then well washed before placing into the box immediately prior to despatch.

UNUSUAL BEHAVIOUR

We have discovered that some Splendids, along with many other forms of animals and birds, possess this strange attitude almost of self-love and have no need or desire for the companionship of their own kind. Even when in a mixed group they will completely shun all contact, keeping completely to themselves and proving utterly useless for breeding. (They are the complete opposite to the "bully boys" which will hold a perch or section of the aviary, make it their territory and ferociously defend it against all comers.) These benign but solitary birds would make a very good choice for anyone desiring a single pet, as quite often they will attach themselves to people. A similar situation can arise when any bird or animal is hand-reared from a very early age and, after a while, it will look upon the person feeding and caring for it as its own parent and believe itself also to be human.

We heard recently of a lamb that had been hand-reared and brought up in a large run with a group of hens. Each night it would not settle down unless it went into the henhouse and slept upon the wide perches with the poultry. We ourselves once owned a golden pheasant cock who never bred or displayed to the hens in his flight, but would do so with great vigour to the lawnmower every time we entered the pen to cut the grass. The golden pheasant hens accompanying him did tend to get very disgruntled and frustrated!

When we first started breeding Splendids we had a pair in an aviary attached to an old stone building and, shortly after the pair were introduced to their new home, the hen disappeared. We assumed she had somehow escaped and, as we could not afford to replace her, the cock was left on his own. There was a doorway from the flight into the building with an old wooden lintel over it. This must have been partly rotten at one end, and the hen Splendid, we later discovered, had made a small entrance in the wide-open joints between the stones and worked away on the lintel, out of sight. She reared four little jewels in that dark, dank hole and, after what appeared to be a lifetime to us, they all appeared to sit on the perches alongside a very proud Mum and Dad!

VARIATION OF COLOURS

Before you purchase your Splendids, visit as many breeders as possible and decide whether you wish to specialise in one particular colour of birds or keep a variation of colours. Where space is not a problem and you have many cages or aviaries at your disposal, it will make no real difference how many varieties are kept, as you will have plenty of room in which to keep all your young Splendids until they have moulted and you are able to select those which will be of most use to you in your breeding programme.

However, if you possess only one or two aviaries or cages, then we feel that you must specialise if you intend to create a strain of your own. Room would have to be found in which to house your selected young until they have fully developed and, if any of them surpass your adults in quality, then obviously these will be kept as your breeding stock for the following year and the adults disposed of.

If you specialise with only one colour, e.g. normals, then you will experience little or no difficulty in up-grading your Splendids, but if you have a variety of colours, then with a small breeding establishment, it will prove to be much more difficult. Sometimes two or more people will form a partnership, sharing expenses and, with a larger unit between them, it will be much easier to create a strain of their own of various colours and types.

VENTILATION

All birdrooms must have a system for ventilation. This does not need to be an elaborate affair with the use of electric fans, although this is very desirable in a large establishment during very hot weather. Rodent and other vermin-proof adjustable ventilators must be fixed, either low in the walls or even in the wooden floor, with others affixed high up or in the ceiling. In this way a current of air can flow by natural convection through the birdroom, creating a lively atmosphere, instead of an oxygen-depleted "fug", which is so often the case.

Even on the coldest days, and if you are using heat, some ventilation will be required as disease is able to spread far more easily in an unventilated, warm and still atmosphere than in one that is well-ventilated with a reasonable movement of air. Roof ventilators, which incorporate a wind or electrically-driven fan, are ideal for use on those occasional stifling hot days we occasionally experience. In our part of the country, Gloucestershire, we do not really have a need for them in our modest birdrooms. We are able to throw open doors and windows and allow the air to flow freely right throughout the buildings. Any birds which are kept in heated and inadequately-vented birdrooms throughout the winter are liable to contract chills and other illnesses when given access to outside aviaries during spells of reasonable weather.

VISITING LARGE ESTABLISHMENTS

On occasions owners of large establishments containing Splendids and other members of the Grass Parrakeet family will allow visits by members of a bird Club or specialist Society. These are generally organised by a Club Secretary or other offical and members of the party are requested to treat the premises visited with respect.

These establishments often consist of some quite rare and valuable specimens and, if an occasion should ever arise for you to join in one of these visits, you would be very wise to do so. If any children are allowed to accompany you, please keep them with you as some unaccompanied children could, by their natural boisterousness, cause damage or losses among some of the more nervous birds. If this should happen, through whatever cause, then it is highly probable that the owner of the establishment would no longer allow visitors.

The information which may be gleaned from the owners of any such establishment mentioned above would be invaluable to anyone proposing to set up even a modest breeding unit and would, no doubt, do much towards alleviating many unexpected setbacks that could be experienced during the early days. Don't ever be nervous about asking a fellow fancier any questions, as we are all only too willing to help if we can.

WATER

The mineral content of water varies throughout the whole country, from soft water areas with a small amount of dissolved minerals, to the very hard water areas where the mineral content is almost at saturation point. This can be observed as "scale" on the inside of kettles and, in our area, it becomes encrusted through evaporation on the insides of our water containers. It is possible that Splendids may be adversely affected by the water if they have been born and bred in an area where the water is soft, for example, and then moved to another where they encounter very hard water. People are also affected by such moves, quite often whilst on holiday, and can suffer tummy upsets.

Various methods of supplying water to Splendids and other stock have been tried. Some fanciers only use boiled water at all times; others will only use rain, or water collected from a clear, mountain stream. We use water from the tap and, although we are in a typical hard water area, it seems to have no ill effect upon our Splendids. Perhaps the addition of the soluble minerals to their diet may even have a beneficial effect. All water is offered to our birds twice daily, in open dishes, which the birds also use for bathing. Drinkers are only used on special occasions, such as for a sick Splendid, or whilst the birds are undergoing show training.

WINTERING SPLENDIDS

All our birds are over-wintered in separate enclosures for cocks and hens, each with an indoor flight and access to an outdoor one during the day. The only times when our birds are not allowed out into the external aviaries are on very cold, foggy days when everywhere is saturated with a clammy mist. These days are very few and far between and the relatively short periods being kept undercover have no adverse effects on our Splendids when they are again allowed to exercise in the open air. A good seed mixture is fed, containing all the warming and fattening seeds required, until the time approaches to fine them down once again for the commencement of the breeding season.

WIRING IN AVIARIES AND BIRDROOMS

Make certain that all wiring in any exposed situation where the Splendids normally or accidentally acquire access, is enclosed inside a plastic or metal trunking, to prevent your birds from chewing on the soft, plastic-sheathed cables and exposing the bare wires, with tragic results.

Hen Splendids have been observed clinging to cables for support, whilst the little carpenters attempt to chew holes in the walls to which the wiring was attached! Any hen approaching breeding condition will attempt to create a nest-hole in the side walls of her shelter or birdroom if no nest-box is available to work in so, when designing your wiring diagram, try if possible to situate the trunking where the birds will be unable to obtain a grip upon it and begin their excavations.

WORMING YOUR SPLENDIDS

This will vary with the location of your birds, whether they are in outside uncovered aviaries with earth floors where the wild bird droppings could very soon re-infest the floor, no matter what is done to treat it, or whether the Splendids are housed in birdrooms with little or no contact with wildings. Whatever system you employ, do not under any circumstances, worm your adult birds whilst they are rearing young, or we feel sure you could end up losing all the babies, as the dosage of worm-destroying chemicals will vary with the size of the individual bird.

Some people advocate worming about every two months, as a precautionary measure but, in our opinion, unless the birds are kept on highly-infested earth floors, this is undesirable. We do not like the idea of continually dosing our Splendids with drugs of any kind, unless there is a specific need to do so. Our system is to give our Splendids a dose of between 0.1-0.2ml of 2.5% *Panacur*, correctly mixed and prescribed for us by our

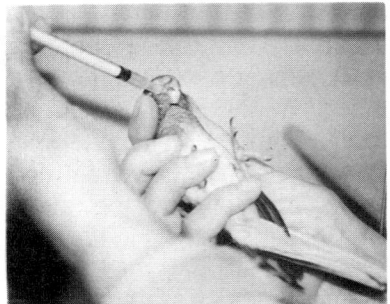

specialist veterinary practitioner. The mixture is drawn into a 1.0ml syringe and, with the Splendid held gently but securely in one hand, the liquid is introduced slowly into the rear corner of its beak. Our birds do not object to the taste and the medicant soon disappears. Live worms could be in the droppings and it would require magnification of around 200 times to be sure of identification. If discovered, a second dose would be advisable 15 days after the first, to kill off any second generation infestation.

Some methods of treatment utilise a short length of thin rubber or plastic tube attached to the syringe and this tube is fed through the beak, directly into the crop. If this is attempted, great care should be taken and a knowledge of anatomy must be acquired, because of the real hazard of the tube entering the bird's lung instead of the crop, resulting in certain death. Our Splendids are in no way upset by our methods and are immediately joined by their mates in the breeding units. We have never yet seen a worm of any kind passed from our birds and, even if any eggs were ejected onto the newspaper floor, they would be removed with the paper within a very short time, thereby decreasing any chance of the birds being re-infected once again.

If you are unsure regarding the treatment for worms in your Splendids, you could request that your birds be treated by their present owner before you purchase them and possibly ask them to show you how the operation is carried out. Having been shown how to do it will make you a little more confident, if and when you decide to conduct the operation yourself. On occasions such as Bird Club meetings, together with the demonstration of bird-washing, nail clipping and other activities, you may be able to obtain the services of a Parrakeet breeder to demonstrate the art of treating for worms. Other materials for worming birds are available besides the one we use, and your vets may prescribe them, but make sure they mix them for you in the correct dosage to treat a bird the size of a Splendid Grass Parrakeet.

Perennial Sow Thistle
(*Sonchus arvensis*)

"X-FACTOR"

This is that indefinable something which can make one person successful in a chosen field while another, operating in exactly the same manner, will fail. Some people have an aura about them which enables them to become accepted by almost any species of bird or animal they come into contact with. They would appear to indulge in a complete rapport or relationship with their stock and the stock show this by their behaviour and breeding successes.

Some of us, unfortunately, are at the other end of the spectrum and appear to create almost the opposite effect but, luckily, very few of us possess the misfortune to unwittingly arouse resentment or even animosity from our charges. The vast majority of us are between these two extremes and, with a little effort on our part, are soon accepted by our Splendids and their families and, if we behave ourselves, will become their firm friends and *confidantes*. There is very little that gives us greater pride and pleasure than to have our Splendids so sure of their safety with us that they will wait near the entrance to their compartments and, on the opening of the door, will jump onto the food tray and inspect our offerings, even before we place them in the cage.

YOUNG

Young Splendids and young people need encouragement to enable them all to gain confidence in each other. The young Splendids, if training commences early enough, can be taught not to fear human contact and their attitude at this time will be with them all their lives. However, if they are hurt or frightened, even accidentally, it will need a lot of patience and could take quite a long time for them to regain their previous trust in their master or mistress.

Young children need a similar attitude shown towards them and, if they show an interest in aviculture, we must all foster this vital concern because - as in days gone by - the young people of today will, we trust, take our places in the years to come and, whilst keeping the hobby alive and thriving, will continue to pass their knowledge onto future generations of youngsters.

ZOOS & BIRD GARDENS

Visits to the above are ideal for originally creating an interest in people's minds for general aviculture and any time that can be spent in conversation with the various keepers attending to the birds will be well spent, as one can acquire a great deal of practical knowledge from them. We have yet to meet any of the attendants unwilling to impart information, but please do not hinder them while they are busy with their charges, although you might observe which foodstuffs are being offered.

Many of us had our interest kindled in birds in this way and passed through the various stages in aviculture, before appreciating that the little gems we are now so involved with were within our capabilities to keep and enjoy.

At these establishments you are able to see the different types of aviaries and smaller cages. From these examples, select the features which please you most and which will fit into both your pockets and your gardens. You will also have rejected some ideas which may have taken a long time to experiment with. New foods and medicants are being developed all the time and these will be used in many of the avicultural establishments, enabling us all to observe the results of their use and helping us to decide which, if any, could be used with advantage during our own breeding undertakings.

ZEST

This is the keen interest and enjoyment we all experience in our involvement with our Splendids, despite the little setbacks we all have to endure. We all get a little disappointed on occasions when things do not proceed as we would wish but, if our Splendids laid six eggs, then hatched and reared six young every time they bred, with nothing ever going amiss, the hobby would possibly lose some of its appeal, especially for those among us with the zeal and eagerness to achieve their aims, whatever they may be, and against all odds. My wife and I hope you have enjoyed this book and find the narration of experiences within of assistance. We wish you all many happy years with your Splendids and, if the book gives you half as much pleasure to read as we obtained in writing it, we will have achieved our objective.

DEDICATION

To David, and to Blue,
for their active encouragement
in making the production
of this book possible.